HORSE OWNERS HANDBOOK

A Practical Guide by LESLEY ECCLES

Editor: Sally Pearson
Designer: Robert Bryant
Typeset by: Kettering Phototypesetters, Northants.
Printed by: Pindar Print, Scarborough.

Horse Owners Handbook

First published in the UK by Emap Books/Windward imprints
respectively owned by Emap National Publications Ltd, Bushfield
House, Orton Centre, Peterborough, PE2 0UW and W H Smith and
Sons Ltd., trading as W.H.S. Distributors, St Johns House, East Street,
Leicester LE9 6NE.

© 1985

ISBN No. 1-85096-006-2

HORSE OWNERS HANDBOOK

1. BUYING YOUR HORSE

Owning a horse or pony opens up a whole new world — you can ride whenever you want, take part in competitions and generally have lots of fun and enjoyment. At the same time however, you have the responsibility of looking after your horse.

This is a daily task which cannot be neglected. If you want to go on holiday you must first make arrangements for your horse's welfare. It's no fun going down to the field when you're suffering from flu either. You might find someone willing to look after your cat or dog for a weekend but a horse is a different matter.

If you're really sure that you want the commitment — in both time and money — then a little forward planning will help you choose your horse.

● Think about where you're going to keep the new arrival. If you do not have your own stable or field then you'll have to rent them or put your horse in livery ie. pay someone else to look after him.

The facilities you have will affect the type of animal you can buy. If you only have a field a native pony will be quite happy living out all year round but this wouldn't be practical with a thoroughbred which needs a stable's comfort.

● By finding somewhere to keep your horse you'll also have an idea of the 'running' costs. Usually it's the weekly feed and grazing bills which put a strain on the bank balance rather than the initial outlay of buying the animal.

● Investigate insurance costs before you buy. As soon as the horse is yours it's wise to have him covered by an insurance policy.

● Allow yourself the cost of having the horse vetted in your 'buying budget'. Ring your vet and ask what he'll charge for this service. It's a sensible precaution to have a prospective purchase looked over by a vet — it could save you from acquiring a sick horse and large veterinary bills.

● Other costs worth including in your buying budget are: 'flu and tetanus vaccinations; grooming kit; headcollar and lead rope; saddle and bridle; worming powders; feed and water buckets; hay nets; costs of transporting the horse to your field and feed.

As soon as you buy a horse you'll need all these unless he's in full livery, when buckets and feed will be supplied.

As you can see, there's more to buying a horse than simply handing over cash.

Your riding ability

Before thinking any more about your horse it's time to stand back and take a look at your riding abilities and ambitions.

Talk to your instructor as an experienced person is better able to judge your talents — human nature being what it is you might have a rather over-optimistic vision of your riding skill.

There's little point in over-horsing yourself. A flashy, always-on-its-toes animal may look impressive but if you cannot handle it you'll soon have regrets.

Consider too what sort of riding activities you'd like to be involved in. If hacking is your pleasure it does not matter if your prospective partner isn't a threat to the Ryan's Sons of the world. However, if a child's main love is gymkhana games then a plodder will not fit the bill at all.

Every horse or pony has its forté — don't expect them to be brilliant at everything. Of course there are some excellent all round performers but the demand for them is high and their price usually reflects this.

Finding a Horse

All over the country there are plenty of horses and ponies for sale: your problem is deciding which is the right one for you.

Don't just rush out and buy the first one you see because you're eager to have your own.

With the help of an experienced person consider your ability, the height, age, conformation and type of pony. Young animals are usually cheaper to buy but unless you have the time to wait for them to mature, the knowledge and experience to deal with youngsters properly, then you should not buy them.

Do not be afraid of buying an animal in his early teens — often they are ideal for first ponies as they have the experience to help their riders, to give novices confidence and, providing they are well looked after, plenty of years of service. A schoolmaster can be a superb introduction to riding and horse ownership, irrespective of your age.

Life with a first horse is much more pleasant if the animal is good in the stable, easy to box, shoe, catch and is traffic proof. If you're buying for a child a bombproof pony is essential. Problems with horses or ponies in traffic can happen easily and they soon destroy a rider's confidence.

Where to Buy

Sales

Do not be tempted to buy from a sale. You do not have the chance to try the horse properly and even for an experienced person, choosing the right pony is a risky business.

Dealers

Many people are suspicious of dealers yet this could be your best chance of finding the horse you want. A reputable dealer will do his best to satisfy your request, providing of course you are not asking the impossible!

You may have to pay a little more but, with the dealer who makes his living from sending customers away happy, you should be able to exchange your animal if it proves unsuitable within a reasonable time limit from the purchase date.

Beware the people who do a little dealing on the side. Their livelihoods do not depend on their good names.

Ask horsey friends if they can recommend a dealer

and if they have been satisfied with the animals they've bought from him.

In a dealer's yard you will be able to try the horse and there should be a choice of suitable animals in your price range. From the beginning tell the dealer what you're after and the price limits.

Riding Schools

Quite a few schools sell horses to their clients and at least you will have had the opportunity to ride the animal regularly and will know, or be able to find out, how it behaves in the stable, whether it can be caught and so on.

However, it's worth remembering that once away from the school environment the horse or pony may change. On their own they may be more lively or they could be rather nappy and unwilling to go forward without the company of their friends.

Buying from Friends

Once again you should know the history of the pony if you buy from a friend. Be honest with yourself — are you the same standard rider as your friend? If not problems may occur which could in turn lead to a lost friendship. Make sure too that you know exactly why the pony is being sold.

Local Clubs

Contact your local Pony or Riding Club secretaries as they often know if any animals are up for sale. You are likely to have seen the horses in action too at local shows so you have an idea of their ability.

Advertisements

If you look through the columns of the local newspaper or horsey magazines you'll see horses for sale.

From the adverts it would seem that each pony is an absolute gem not to be missed but the reality can be completely different. It's worth noting what isn't said as much as what is included.

Ring up and ask about the pony. Why is it being sold? How good is it in traffic? Is it good to box, shoe and catch? Do they clip it in winter — if not, why? Is it because he's difficult to clip? Have they had any problems with the pony? What illnesses or injuries has it had? Who rides it and how often? What bit do they ride it in? What competitions has it done and how successfully? What's the asking price? Is it open to a vet?

You may not get totally honest answers to everything but at least you'll get an idea of the pony and whether it's worth going to have a look at it. Most caring owners are concerned that their ponies go to good homes so don't be surprised if some questions are asked of you too.

Trying a horse or pony

The first priority when you go to look at a pony is to take someone with you who has bought horses before and whose judgement you can trust. They will be able to advise you.

Watch how the pony behaves in the stable — is he friendly, nervous or bad-tempered? Ask to see him tacked up — does he accept the bridle or make life

Letting the owner ride the pony first gives you the chance to see how it behaves on the flat and over jumps.

difficult by throwing his head up, zooming around the stable and so on.

Don't be too eager to ride the pony yourself. Let the owner ride it first and then you can see how it moves and behaves. Ask them to walk, trot, canter and jump him for you — make sure they jump the pony going away from the field gate too as the pony's more likely to play up then.

If the jumps were already set up when you arrived move and rebuild one or two — the pony may have been jumped over the existing course several times. Give him something new and see how he reacts. It's especially important to find out the pony's attitude to jumping if you are keen on entering show jumping classes.

Let the owner ride him in traffic for you too. You can then try the pony and see how you get on together. If you're still interested ask to see the pony loaded and see if you can catch him in a field.

Presuming that your adviser thinks he's okay as far as soundness, conformation and temperament goes, and you think he's the pony for you, ask if you can have him on a week's trial.

You'll probably find that people are more willing to let ponies out on trial than horses. A trial gives you the chance to get to know the pony better and decide whether you are going to be suited. Naturally though an owner may be reluctant to agree to a trial because you might send the pony back in a week and he could be injured or spoiled in some way.

It's also possible that the owners may ask you to leave a small deposit as a token of your good intentions.

If you decide to buy the pony tell the owners you wish to have him, subject to your vet passing the pony as satisfactory. Then arrange for a vetting and try to be present yourself. Explain to your vet what sort of activities you intend to do with your pony, he will then examine the animal thoroughly and advise you whether it is fit for your needs.

Vetting

If you're about to spend your hard earned cash on a horse it makes sense to check that the horse is healthy and suitable for the work you intend it to do.

You can do this by having your horse vetted — but what does the vet do during this process and why? If you can be present when your prospective purchase is vetted there's a lot you can learn.

Each vet will develop his own system of looking at a horse but he will cover the following areas:

● A general view will give an idea of the horse's condition and whether he is a nervous type. With a grey a check will be made under the tail for any signs of melanomas — a skin cancer they are prone to.

● The head and face are examined for swellings, tooth troubles, sinusitis and facial paralysis which may follow a blow. The horse's eyesight is checked and the eyes and nostrils checked for any discharge.

● By looking at the teeth the vet can tell the horse's age and also whether there are any signs of crib biting or missing teeth which may make eating difficult or uncomfortable.

● The throat is checked for any evidence of a hobday operation or tubing.

● The crest of the neck and withers are examined for swellings, sores, or sweet itch.

● The back is inspected for sores and warbles. By looking at the development of the muscles on back, loin and quarters the vet can tell whether one side has been favoured, possibly because of an injury or a strain.
To test for stiffness or pain the vet runs a

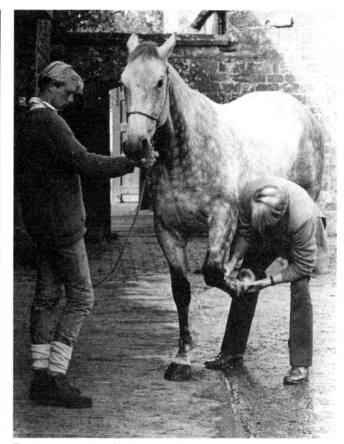

During a vetting the horse's legs are examined with particular attention paid to the tendons and joints.

9

thermometer case firmly along the back, beside the spine from withers to tail. The horse will squirm but hopefully without showing any pain, if he does then there is a problem which the vet may investigate further.

● The front legs will be examined. The vet looks to see if they are straight. Does the horse have knock knees, bow legs, pigeon toes or splay feet? Is he back or over at the knee?

The legs are carefully felt, first with the leg straight and then flexed. Careful attention is paid to the joints, tendons and coronet.

Circling the horse will reveal any lameness problems.

The hoof walls are looked at for signs of ringbone, sidebone or any cracks and ridges. Underneath the hoof the sole and frog are examined.

● In the same way the hindlegs are examined with special attention being paid to the hocks for signs of weakness, spavin or thoroughpin.

● The vet will ask to see the horse moving — first at the walk and then the trot, moving away from and towards him, then having the horse circled in both directions.

This gives him the chance to note the horse's action and look for any signs of lameness.

● Heart and lungs are tested. An occasional missed heart beat is quite common while the horse is at rest but if this continues when the horse works it can be significant.

● The vet will watch the horse being ridden in trot and canter, observing the horse's movement and reactions to the rider. The heart and lungs are then checked again.

● The rider will be asked to gallop the horse passing fairly close to the vet so that he can hear any unusual breathing noises. The vet will again listen to heart and lungs for any sign of trouble.

● After galloping the horse is left for a while before the vet checks for any stiffness or lameness. Finally the prospective purchaser will be advised as to the suitability of the horse.

Arrange for your insurance cover so that as soon as the horse is yours he is insured.

Money

Before you look at a pony you'll know whether it is in your price range or not. Naturally you'd expect to negotiate a final price rather than simply accepting the asking price. Whoever you buy from will want the whole amount before handing over the animal.

Some of you may be tempted to take out a loan to cover the cost of buying your first horse. Unless you can easily afford the repayment plus the cost of keeping your horse plus any unexpected bills such as veterinary fees and of course still be able to pay your own living expenses, you'd be wise to wait and save.

The cost of keeping a horse is enough without the added worry of a loan repayment.

Prices of animals vary throughout the country and according to their breeding, their age, achievements and size. As the cost of keeping a horse usually increases in winter it is possible to buy animals a little cheaper at this time of year — but of course you will have to find the money for the extra feed etc.

Keep a check on prices in your area by noting the amounts asked in adverts and those fetched at sales.

Insurance

With such a variety of insurance policies for horses finding one to suit your needs and pocket can be quite a task. It's worth talking to other horse owners and discussing how various firms have reacted when claims have been made. You may be warned off certain companies or have a decent one recommended.

It's a good idea to shop around and find out what is offered. Try to find a policy which is aimed at horses — the firm hopefully has a better understanding of the problems involved.

To get a good selection of policies ask an insurance broker for advice. This does not cost anything and they should have a number of policies for comparison. If there is anything you do not understand on a proposal form ring the company concerned and discuss it with them.

It is worth taking this extra time and trouble because if you make a claim and something goes wrong you'll hate yourself for not double checking the small print.

As you investigate policies you'll see some offer selective insurance while others come on a package basis. The latter usually covers death of the horse, loss of use, theft or straying, vet's bills, tack, personal accident and public liability.

Selective policies mean you can start, say, with death and loss of use of the horse and then add other sections as you think fit. As a member of the British Horse Society you automatically have third party public liability cover as well as personal accident insurance.

The loss of use section needs close scrutiny — some firms will not pay 100 per cent of the horse's value if you decide to keep him alive as a companion for light riding following an accident. What would your insurance company do if your horse was insured for showing and was then blemished so he could no longer be shown? Would they pay out on the loss of use? ASK before you insure with them.

With vet's fees it's usual for you to pay the first £25

or so — check the excess amount which applies to your insurance. Find out the claim procedure too — some firms want notification that the horse is receiving treatment immediately. It's all too easy to forget to do this when your horse is ill but it could mean you have to fight to get your fees paid.

If your horse is an older animal you'll find insurance companies will arrange cover at a higher rate. The age when these rates apply can vary, sometimes it's 12, other companies use 15 as the changeover point. Shopping around can save money. A

Freezemarking is a sensible precaution — these numbers will appear white when the hair grows back.

certificate from your vet may be needed — this will be at your expense.

As you fill in your proposal form you have to declare which activities your horse will be involved in. Keep a note of them for yourself so that you are always sure that the horse is covered for the particular activity you have in mind. If you decide to do something different which is not included, notify the company immediately and pay the extra premium.

Any details on your form which are found to be inaccurate eg. omitting to mention previous illnesses or claims, will invalidate the policy and you'll have wasted your money.

There's not much point in putting an unrealistic value on your horse either — most companies agree to pay the sum insured or market value whichever is the lesser. If you over value your horse you only increase your premium and to no purpose.

Safety Measures

Apart from insurance you may wish to have your pony freeze marked. This means that his hair is clipped away over a small patch about six inches in length (perhaps where the saddle goes or on his neck) and then a number is branded onto him. It is quite painless. You have registration papers for the pony and these are passed on when the pony is sold, with the new owner being noted. This acts as a deterrent to horse thieves and some insurance companies offer reduced premiums for freeze marked animals.

The firm who does this freeze branding is Farmkey

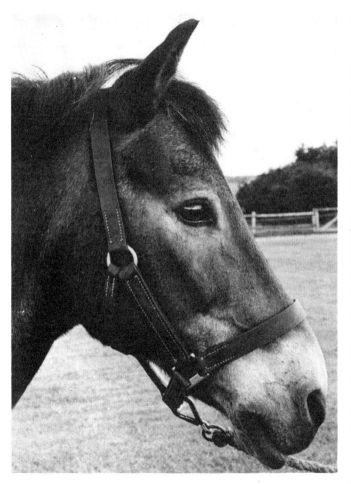

of Banbury, Oxfordshire. It's a precaution worth taking, especially if your pony lives out all year in a field.

Having your pony branded in this way costs less if a group of friends get together and have their ponies marked at the same time. You may find that your local riding club will also organise a freeze branding session.

It is also worth padlocking your field gate to deter or at least hinder thieves. Mark your tack too as stealing horse equipment can be quite profitable.

Conformation

No horse is perfect but some have better conformation — or shape — than others. When you are looking for a horse you should be aware of the good and bad points of an animal as poor conformation can make a horse more susceptible to injury or disease.

Ideally you should take an experienced person with you to view a horse you are thinking of buying but there is no harm in looking at other horses — perhaps those at your riding school or belonging to friends — with a more critical eye.

The points you should look at are:

Head: This should be in proportion to the rest of the horse's body, with well placed, alert ears and bright, large eyes. There should be plenty of width between the eyes, the muzzle should be well defined and the nostrils

LEFT: A kind looking pony — the eyes are bright and his ears show that he's taking an interest.

large. Look at the horse's teeth — if the lower teeth are behind the upper the animal has a parrot mouth which will make it more awkward for him to graze properly.

Neck: The shape of the neck will affect the head carriage so it should not be too straight or heavy. If the head is set on the neck at too acute an angle it may restrict the breathing.

Shoulders: A horse with a good sloping shoulder will be a more comfortable ride. There should be a good slope from the point of the shoulder to the withers so helping the shock absorber effect to the front legs.

Withers: Should be well defined, tapering away gently to give a wide surface so that the saddle does not sink down.

Back: You've probably heard the phrases 'a nice short back' or 'long backed', the latter possibly being used in a slightly derogatory way. A shorter back is usually associated with strength — after all the rider's weight is carried on the back — but the subject is open to argument. Horses which are stayers are likely to have long backs. Many people do not mind a long backed horse providing he is well ribbed up — the space between the last rib and the point of hip is not more than a couple of inches.

Loin and Quarters: The loins, which should be short and strong, are very vulnerable as they are the least supported part of the horse's back. No doubt you've heard a horse's hindquarters described as his 'engine'

— therefore they need to be strong, reaching well down into the second thighs.

Girth: A good deep girth means the horse has plenty of room for his heart and lungs.

Front Legs: If you look at a horse from the front and his legs appear to be too close together, or to use a popular expression they 'come out of the same hole' then the horse is narrow chested. The area for his heart and lungs is therefore less and forelegs which are close together may lead to brushing. The knees should be broad, flat and evenly placed — look at the bone of the forearm and the cannon from the front, they should be in a straight line with the knee evenly positioned. If this line is not continuous then an uneven strain is put on the knee.

Short, strong cannon bones with clearly defined tendons behind them are ideal. Many advertisements for horses say 'good bone' — this refers to the measurement of the cannon bone immediately beneath the knee.

'Over at the Knee' means that the knee is permanently bent. In old horses it may be as a result of wear, the back tendons becoming contracted but it can also be seen in young horses.

The term 'back at the knee' refers to a much more serious fault as the forelegs show a slightly concave line from the forearm to the fetlock joint. Undue strain is therefore thrown on the back tendons.

Hind legs: Thighs should be long and well muscled with the second thigh or gaskin in particular needing to be strong. This is because the muscular portion of the tendons which activate the hock and foot originate in this area.

Hocks, when seen from the side, should be virtually square in shape. The point of the hock should be well defined otherwise there will be greater strain on the curb ligament. If the hocks turn inwards when seen from the back the horse is cow hocked — a sign of weakness. Hocks which turn slightly outwards usually denote strength.

Pasterns: Should be at a gentle angle — the more upright it is the less the pastern acts as a buffer against concussion. Pasterns which slope too much put more strain on the ligaments and tendons.

Hoof: Needs to be deep with a good width between the heels and a well developed frog. There should not be any marked rings or grooves on the horn.

Horses with turned out toes are likely to brush, though turned in toes are not considered to be a bad fault.

Teeth

If you want to know a horse's age people will tell you to look at his teeth — which is fine providing you know what to look for!

Judging a horse's age is a skilled business but with a knowledge of how a horse's teeth grow and develop you can make a fair assessment. Recognising the signs does take practice and experience but it is something you can start to do at your riding school before buying your own horse.

Horses have two types of teeth — the incisors used for grazing and the molars used for grinding food. A horse with a 'full mouth' has six incisors on the top and bottom jaws and six molars on each side of both jaws. We use the incisors as indicators of the horse's age.

Behind the corner incisors are the canine teeth or tushes. These usually only appear in males, pushing through when the horse is about four. Further back on the upper jaw wolf teeth may appear but not all horses have them.

Wolf teeth are often removed as they have virtually no roots and serve no purpose. If anything they can be a hindrance as they may interfere with the action of the bit, causing the horse to evade it.

By the time he's nine months old a foal will have a set of milk teeth which are small and white. Permanent teeth are much larger and a yellowish colour.

Two and a Half Years: The first four permanent incisors appear, the central two in each jaw pushing through and being in wear by the time the horse is three.

Three and a Half Years: The lateral incisors come through — these replace the milk teeth on either side of the central incisors.

Five Years: By this time the corner incisors are through and in wear so the horse has all his permanent teeth. As the corners have only just pushed through the tables, or surfaces of the teeth, only meet at the front.

Six Years: The corner teeth have worn level, all the tables of the incisors are in use and level.

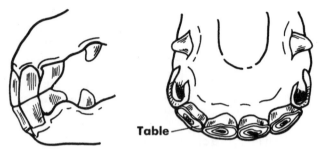

By five years the horse has all his permanent teeth but the tables of the corner teeth only meet at the front.

To help us age a horse who is over six we use the mark which is in the centre of the tooth's wearing surface. This is known as the cup or infundibulum and it disappears with age. Together with the shape of the teeth and Galvayne's Groove they act as age indicators.

Seven Years: The cups on the central incisors are less

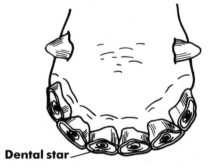

Dental stars appear around the age of eight.

distinct and a hook develops on the back of the corner incisor in the upper jaw.

Eight Years: The hook disappears, the cups on the laterals have worn out and on the central incisors a mark known as a dental star appears. This is a dark line between the now faint outline of the cup and the front of the tooth.

If you see a horse described as 'aged' it usually means he's over eight.

Nine Years: The dental star appears on the lateral incisors too, the cups having all but disappeared. A nine-year-old hook now develops.

Nine or 10 Years: Galvayne's Groove appears — this is on the outer surface of the tooth and is a dark line which starts from the gum.

10 to 15 Years: By 10 years old the cups have disappeared, the dental star is on all teeth and the shape of the teeth start to change. The tables become more triangular and from now on the horse's teeth start to slope more and more.

15 Years: Galvayne's Groove increases by about an eighth of an inch each year so by 15 the groove is usually about halfway down the tooth and by 20 years the groove extends the whole length of the tooth.

Teeth Care

A horse's teeth need regular attention. The molars,

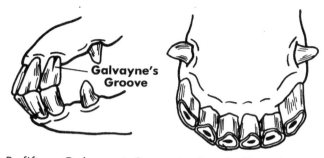

By fifteen Galvayne's Groove is about halfway down the tooth — note how the tables of the teeth have become more triangular.

Roof of mouth

Upper molar teeth

Lower molar teeth

Cross section of tongue

Sloping grinding surfaces of teeth

Lower jaw

This cross section of a horse's mouth shows the sloping grinding surfaces of the teeth which need regular attention.

which do the grinding work, have sloping surfaces and often the inside edges of the lower teeth become sharp. They can cut and scratch the tongue while the outside edges of the upper molars, if also allowed to become rough, affect the cheeks.

Ask your vet to check you horse's teeth when he comes out on his annual visit to give the horse his booster injections. In between times you can check the teeth yourself — hold the horse's tongue out of the side of his mouth and then rub your fingers along the molars. Another tell tale sign that something is wrong is quidding — when the horse drops partly ground food onto the floor.

If the teeth need attention your vet will rasp them. A gag may be used to keep the mouth open while the rasp is moved backwards and forwards to remove sharp edges. It does not normally take very long and is not unpleasant for the pony.

Colours and Markings

At some point you'll need to declare your pony's colour and markings — for instance if you register him to take part in affiliated competitions — so how do you tell the difference between a sock and stocking, a dark bay and a black?

To decide on your pony's true colour look at his points — these are the tips of his ears, mane, tail, legs and his muzzle. For instance a true black pony will have a black muzzle.

The four main colours of horses are bay, brown, chestnut and black. White is not a colour as such but shows a lack of pigmentation, grey results from pigmentation failure or variation.

As grey horses grow older their coats become lighter, often ending up white. However, the only true white horses are albinos who have pink rather than grey skin and pale blue eyes.

Foals do not usually stay the colour they are born — by the time they are two and a half the adult colour has established itself.

Black — horse is black in colour with black points.

Brown — dark brown or nearly black in colour but with brown points.

Bay — brown coloured horses with black points.

Chestnut — ginger or reddish colour with similar mane and tail. May be light, dark or liver chestnut.

Grey — both black and white hairs occur throughout the coat. With iron grey horses the black is pronounced, with a light grey the white hairs predominate. Fleabitten greys have dark hairs but they occur in tufts.

Dun — ancient and native breeds are often dun. Colour varies from a mousy to golden, with black points and zebra marks on the limbs or a dark line along the back, called a dorsal stripe.

Roans — could be strawberry, bay or blue colour, showing a mixture of chestnut or bay and white, or black and white hairs throughout the coat.

Piebald — large irregular patches of white and black.

Skewbald — large irregular patches of white and any other colour except black.

Palomino — golden colour coat with very light, almost white, mane and tail.

Markings:

Star — any white mark on the forehead, no matter what shape it is.

Stripe — a narrow white line running down the length of the face.

Blaze — a broader band of white down the face which extends over the bones of the nose.

White Face — where a blaze extends over the forehead, eyes, nose and muzzle the horse is said to have a white face.

Snips — small white marks between or on one or other of the nostrils.

Wall Eyes — this is when the colouring of the iris is white or blue-white.

Legs — markings on the legs are usually defined according to the part of the anatomy they cover eg. white heels, fetlocks etc.

Full stocking — this is when the white extends right up the leg. White up to the knee or hock is just a stocking.

Socks — white marking involving the fetlock and part of the cannon bone.

Ermine — term used to describe black spots on white.

18

Native Breeds

A native pony is often recommended as a first buy — they are hardy, useful animals ideal as an introduction to horse ownership. Once experience has been gained and confidence increased, riders, both adult and children, can move on to ponies with more 'blood' in them.

Britain is lucky in having nine native breeds with enough choice to suit both adults and young people.

The Fell, Dales, Welsh Cobs, Connemara, New Forest and Mainland Highland ponies are the bigger breeds.

At one time Fell and Dales ponies were virtually indistinguishable but now the Dales is about two inches bigger and of stockier build.

Originally used as pack ponies both breeds are good all purpose ponies, tough but with lively characters. Fells are about 14hh and Dales 14.2hh — many of the latter are jet black with plenty of fine hair on their heels.

There are four types of Welsh ponies with the cobs being the largest, standing at 14.2hh to 15.2hh. Equally talented under saddle or in harness they are much in demand as all rounders. When crossed with thoroughbreds some super riding animals are produced.

Ireland's representative, the Connemara, is respected for its toughness, intelligence and good nature. The breed society in England recognises a height limit of 14.2hh. Grey is the predominant colour and the ponies should have compact bodies, free action and plenty of bone.

Conditions in Hampshire's New Forest area mean the ponies here have to be hardy with strong constitutions. The New Forest ponies, especially those with more bone, make good riding ponies for both adults and children. Intelligent and resourceful they are also used, like many of our mountain and moorland breeds, for foundation stock.

The Scottish Highlands have the largest and strongest of our native breeds. Docile and sure footed too, there are three types of Highland ponies.

The Mainland ponies stand 14.2hh, there are the popular riding ponies at 13.2hh to 14.2hh and the smallest standing 12.2hh to 13.2hh.

Scotland is also the home of one of the world's smallest pony breeds — the Shetland. With a history revolving around hard work, Shetlands are remarkably strong for their size. They are often used for both riding and driving, the usual height being about 10 hands.

From Exmoor comes Britain's oldest breed. The Exmoors are also incredibly strong — standing about 12.2hh they are capable of carrying a fully grown man. Tough and wilful they make excellent all rounders if handled with kindness and firmness once taken away from their home environment.

Dartmoor ponies are similar to their near neighbours — being compact weight carriers they are suitable for children and small adults. They do not exceed 12.2hh.

The three remaining breeds from Wales are the Welsh Mountain Section A up to 12hh, the Section B up to 13.2hh and Section C which is the Welsh Pony cob type.

All the Welsh breeds have small quality heads, powerful quarters and deep girths. Versatile, kind and intelligent, they are all very popular and highly successful in the show ring:

Other breeds

You'll see various cross bred animals for sale as well as the pure bred animals. Arabs, whether full or part bred, are popular choices. An ancient and beautiful breed it has influenced other breeds throughout the world. Known for their stamina, speed and beauty these horses stand between 14.2hh and 15hh.

Like Arabs, many Thoroughbreds have been used to improve other breeds. Crossed with Welsh Cobs, Irish Draught or hunter types they produce some superb riding horses.

If any particular breed interests you contact the breed society, who will give you details of breeders with horses for sale and dates of any breed sales. The addresses can be found at the back of this book.

Vices

In their wild state horses used kicking, biting, bucking and running off as their methods of defence and survival. These instincts are still strong even though the horse has been domesticated for centuries.

Some of this instinctive behaviour can become a problem through man's bad handling or treatment. Bucking, biting and so on develop into vices.

If you are a new horse owner you probably will not have the experience or knowledge needed to deal with a problem horse.

There are a number of vices you may come across and the following will help you to realise why they happen and what you can do to prevent or cure them. Some vices should only be dealt with by an experienced and competent rider — never hesitate to seek help if you are having difficulties in any case.

Bolting

A heavy handed rider on a sensitive mouthed horse is a recipe for disaster — very often the horse will try to escape the pain by running off. A badly fitting bit or bridle may also hurt a horse and cause him to try to flee to safety.

Too much food and too little exercise may cause an animal to get above himself and take off; nervous horses could be reacting to the rider carrying a whip or wearing spurs for the first time; ponies sometimes simply take charge and zoom off home or back to their friends.

Try and identify the cause and correct it. If you know your horse may take hold be prepared. Always ride him forward on a good contact.

If he does bolt there's no point in just pulling against him as a horse's strength far outmatches that of humans. If you have room try turning him in ever decreasing circles — one problem here is that the bit may be pulled through the mouth.

Try steadying your seat by pressing your knees firmly into the saddle, lean with one hand on the withers and with the other hand make a series of short, sharp

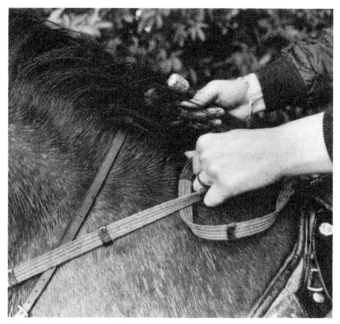

One way to try and regain some control if your horse bolts is to lean with one hand on the withers and with the other hand make short sharp pulls.

pulls. Alternatively fix your hand on the withers and cross the other hand over and down, locking the elbow straight.

If you do have the room one method which seems to work is to let the horse go and when he starts to tire, keep him going on at a gallop. Often it makes horses reluctant to try this trick again. However, if your horse has bolted through genuine fright there's little point in making him continue.

Bucking

Most horses occasionally give a playful buck out of sheer high spirits but when this becomes a regular occurence it's not funny. Letting off steam is one thing but a rodeo performance with the serious intent of dumping the rider is another matter.

If the horse suddenly takes to bucking have a look at his tack — something may be pinching him or causing a sore back. Young horses who are not accustomed to a rider's weight may register a protest by bucking and cold backed horses are also likely to buck.

Watch how a horse reacts when he's tacked up — if he appears to hunch up when the saddle is put on he could be cold backed. With such horses always use a numnah and tack up a good while before you mount.

Too much feed and not enough work can lead to a horse working off his excess energy by bucking so look to these causes too if your horse acquires the habit.

If your horse gives a single buck you have time to remind him with your stick that this behaviour is not on. When a horse gives a series of bucks you're probably too busy staying on to use your stick.

Sit out the bucks as best as you can, trying to stay tall or leaning back a little. If you can raise the horse's head so much the better as he needs to put his head down to buck. When he's finished tell him off, send him forward strongly and make him work hard. If you anticipate a buck keep the horse's head up, use your legs and send him on.

Rearing

This is an extremely dangerous habit which can so easily result in injury to horse and rider. A confirmed rearer is difficult to deal with and you should leave horses like these to experienced riders.

Sometimes a horse will rear or come up halfway out of sheer excitement — perhaps a youngster or a keen pony being counted down at the start of a cross country round, or gymkhana game.

Far more serious though are the horses who really mean to get their own way — they've discovered that rearing is a good method to use.

If you find yourself in the unfortunate position of being on a bad rearer lean forward and to one side. Should you lean back you could bring the horse right over and on top of you. As you lean forward give the horse a loose rein but be prepared to whirl him round in a circle the second his hooves touch the ground.

Keep the horse circling, using your whip at the same time — he cannot rear again when his head and neck are bent. If you hit a horse while he is rearing it will only make him go higher.

Some animals are perfectly fine to ride but rear and lash out in the stable and field. If this is done out of temper or malice rather than fear you would be doing yourself a favour if you sold the horse and bought another. A novice owner can do without the strain of looking after difficult animals.

All horses buck out of high spirits but it can develop into a serious vice.

22

Horses which have been ill treated may use rearing as a method of defence. It takes any horse which has lost its trust in humans a long time to regain confidence. Rebuilding that trust can be very trying — often it's a case of one step forward and three back. You should be aiming to enjoy your first horse as much as possible and without too much hassle — buy carefully.

If you are leading a horse which rears don't pull against him. When he comes down send him forward, using your voice, a flick of the lead rope or whip if you have one, and keep him moving on.

With any rearer check that his teeth or tack are not causing pain.

Shying

You can be riding along quite happily when suddenly the horse sees something he doesn't like or recognise and leaps into the road. It's easy to see that shying — when the horse moves sideways and backwards — can be very dangerous.

Young horses often spook at new sights and sounds — it's all part of their growing up but it will be much safer if you ride a youngster out in the company of older, more experienced companions. They will help his confidence and you too!

Older horses will shy too: something as simple as a newly erected sign on a regular ride can cause it, just because it's different. The best course of action is to let the horse smell or examine the object. He'll need some gentle persuasion to approach it but keep asking him to go forward, talking to him and patting him. If you do this kindly but firmly most horses only take a few minutes to realise that the 'monster' really isn't that bad.

Horses which shy at traffic present more of a problem, especially as hacking out necessitates going on the roads for most of us.

Ride with friends if possible, keeping the more traffic proof ponies, between you and the traffic. Ask motorists to slow down and thank them if they do — they are then more likely to slow down and courtesy costs nothing.

If you have to ride out alone keep to the quieter side roads. By having your horse's head bent slightly inwards as for a circle you can prevent him swinging his hindquarters into traffic.

Try to rent or borrow a field near a busy road as grazing near traffic usually helps an animal to overcome his fear.

Think positively yourself — if you look for objects your horse can spook at or start to tense up every time you hear a car in the distance your horse will wonder why you're nervous and start to get jittery himself.

Regular schooling will help discipline your horse so that he responds to your leg and goes forward when asked. This is advantageous if you feel him becoming tense at the sight of a strange object. Keep your legs on, ease his head away from the peculiar sight, look forwards yourself and the chances are he will not shy.

Stargazing

This is an uncomfortable habit — both for the horse and rider. Usually it's pain in the mouth or back which causes the horse to go about with his head held high, resisting the rider's aids. Riding these horses, with their hollow backs, trailing quarters and awkward head carriage, is not a pleasant experience.

Check the tack and teeth. If no obvious answer lies there ask your vet to check the horse's back. By adopting a high head carriage the animal will have built up the wrong muscles on the underside of the neck so it will take some time to correct the problem and to develop a decent shape.

Ride a stargazer on a loose rein, very quietly, carrying out exercises such as circles, changes of rein and transitions. Encourage the horse to go forward actively, lowering his head and stretching his neck.

Gradually the correct muscles will develop along the top of the neck, those underneath will reduce and a better shape or outline will result.

Head Shaking

Another habit which makes the horse uncomfortable to ride — but it could have developed because the rider is causing the horse pain in the first place.

Rough hands, a bit which is worn and sharp or totally the wrong choice for the horse, a tightly fitting bridle, or toothache can all cause head shaking.

Get some help from an expert if it is your riding ability, have the horse's teeth checked, ride him in a mild bit and let him relax and stretch his muscles.

If, despite this, the habit persists, it's worth asking the vet to check for ear problems.

Kicking

Whether it's people or other horses which are the targets kicking is a serious vice which cannot always be stopped.

Look for the cause — is a stabled horse bored because he spends 23 hours stuck in his box with little to keep him amused? Other causes could be itchy heels, sheer mischievousness, and a mare in season in a nearby box.

If boredom is the root of the problem turn the horse out for some exercise or if that's not possible see if you can split his exercise periods into two, put some toys in his stable to keep him amused — something soft suspended from the roof.

Be prepared is the motto with kickers — tie a red ribbon round their tail when out in company so other riders know to avoid them. Try not to allow yourself to be bunched up in a collecting ring — stay away from others and do not ride into the ring for your class until the last minute.

Mares in season can become unsociable and lash out so keep your distance. The instant any horse attempts to kick punish him — the sooner you curb the habit the better.

Windsucking and crib biting

These are two serious vices as they affect the horse's digestive system, leading to indigestion, and flatulent colic. With crib biting a horse's teeth become unnaturally worn.

When a horse crib bites he takes hold of any solid object with his teeth (the rim of his manger, his stable door), and arching his neck, gulps in air. An expert at this may dispense with the hard surface and simply stand in the stable, gulping air. This is known as windsucking.

Boredom is often the problem. To keep his mind occupied the horse has turned to crib biting and it soon develops into a serious vice — and one which is difficult to cure.

Anti crib biting straps may be fitted — these fasten around the horse's neck and a heavy arched piece of leather or metal for really bad cases presses against the lower part of the windpipe making it difficult to gulp air.

Wire mesh can be fitted on surfaces or nasty smelling and tasting preparations smeared on to discourage the horse from grabbing hold of the edge.

You may see a bit with holes in the mouthpiece — this is a windsucker's bit and is attached to a headcollar and left on all the time, except for feeding and work. It prevents the horse sucking air.

These vices are difficult to cure and an interesting stable routine will certainly help prevent your horse adopting them.

Split up his feeds, turn him out for exercise, give him a hay net to pull at — a stable looking on to a busy yard or road will give him something to look at.

Weaving

This is another vice resulting from boredom and is a sign of unsoundness. The horse stands with his head over the stable door and rocks incessantly from side to side.

As he rocks from one foot to the other he may rub his chest against the door causing soreness. It's a habit which other horses in the yard start to copy too and that's not likely to make you very popular.

Grating with a V-shaped section in the middle through which the horse can look is often fixed to the top door of a weaver's stable. Unfortunately some horses are so determined to continue with their habit that they stand just inside the door, rocking away.

Sometimes, small blocks of wood suspended from the stable door help stop the problem. Every time the horse moves from side to side he knocks himself.

Biting

Luckily confirmed biters who lunge at you savagely are not too common. What starts as a mischievous habit with playful nips can lead to a nasty vice and so firm handling is needed.

Never tease a horse or feed too many tit-bits — you'll only encourage him to investigate every visitor for a treat. When he doesn't find them he may nip.

Some animals are ticklish and may try to nip you while being groomed. Try short racking the horse — ie. tying him up short — to groom him but if this upsets him more you'll have to stay alert ready to dodge his teeth and administer a telling off. Break any biting habit in its early stages rather than allowing the horse to get away with misbehaving — that's how vices develop.

2. GRASS KEPT PONIES

A common method of keeping a pony is to rent a field and turn him out all year round. However, it's not quite as simple as it may sound.

Finding a field can be a problem. Get on your bicycle or in your car and visit local farms, asking if they let grazing or know of anyone who does. Enquire at the local farrier's, saddler's or ask other pony owners. You may see grazing advertised in your local paper. Prices vary but £5 to £10 a week is about average.

You may not even need to rent a field as some livery yards and riding schools offer grass livery i.e. the pony is kept there but lives out at grass.

If you do share or rent a field you must check it is safe for your pony.

What are the advantages of keeping a pony at grass?

Being outdoors and free to wander eating when he pleases, is natural to a horse. He will also be exercising himself to some extent.

How big a field do I need?

For one pony a one and a half acre field is sufficient providing it is good pasture — not full of weeds or knee high tough grass. Try to find a well drained field — if there are places which are always under water or the grazing is not very good you must discount those areas.

With a larger acreage you'll also be able to split the field and 'rest' sections of it.

What shelter will the horses need?

In summer horses will appreciate a shady shelter as relief from flies and heat — in winter it will act as a welcome respite from wind, rain and snow.

Tall, thick hedges provide natural windbreaks but if nothing like this is available a wooden shelter is needed.

Several firms make them and will erect the shelter for you if you cannot manage. Choose a level, well drained site and have the open side away from the prevailing wind.

The entrance needs to be wide and inviting, with a roof high enough so your horse does not feel discouraged from going in. Spread straw inside for extra warmth.

To stop the entrance getting churned into mud spread some rubble around, taking care to remove any sharp objects first. Rubble is also useful near the field gate as this area tends to get very muddy.

What type of water supply is needed?

Water is as essential to life as food so make sure your field has some kind of provision. You may have a natural water supply in the form of a running stream but be careful that the access to it is safe. If it is not, fence it off.

If there is a sandy bottom to the stream you may get

Field shelters such as this will be appreciated in winter and summer.

Troughs such as this are much safer than old baths and less work than buckets.

problems with colic. Stagnant ponds should also be securely fenced off.

A self filling trough is ideal but do not position it too close to a fence or you could get ponies trapped between it and the fencing. Make sure the edges are smooth to reduce the risk of injury to the horse.

You need to check daily that the trough is working correctly and to clear leaves or dirt to prevent clogging.

If you have to use buckets ensure they are cleaned and refilled two or three times a day. Putting the buckets in old tyres will prevent them being knocked over.

Is the fencing safe and adequate?

Good fencing is essential — you do not want your pony trampling down a tatty old fence and wandering around the countryside. It also needs to be safe — avoid barbed wire as the damage this can cause is horrendous.

Post and rail fencing is the best but of course it's also expensive. When you rent a field ask the owner to specify who is responsible for the upkeep of the fences in writing.

To discourage horses from jumping out, the fences need to be a reasonable height — 4ft 6ins is fine. Check there are no gaps which Houdini-like ponies can wriggle through. The bottom strand of plain wire on a fence, or the bottom rail, needs to be high enough to prevent a pony from getting his foot caught over it but also sufficiently low enough to stop a pony from squeezing underneath.

Thick hedges are good but weak areas or gaps must be supplemented with timber. Hedges also offer natural shelter and act as windbreaks.

The field gate should be easy for you to open and close but horse-proof.

Are there any poisonous plants?

Ragwort, yew, ivory, deadly nightshade, hemlock, purple milk vetch, privet, St. John's wort and buckthorn are all harmful or fatal to horses.

If the pasture is poor you'll probably find ragwort which is recognisable by its woody stems and yellow flowers. Pull up any dangerous plants by the roots and burn them. Don't just throw them down as some are more lethal dead than growing.

Ask your instructor, Pony or Riding Club secretary for help if you're not sure about identifying plants.

LEFT: Good post and rail fencing and the company of other horses or animals are two aims you should work towards.

ABOVE: Ragwort is often found on poor pasture.

What other hazards could there be?

Check a prospective field for broken glass, bits of wire, nails etc. When in use make regular searches for any dangerous objects which have been thrown in.

How can I take care of my grazing?

If it's big enough, section off your grazing so that part of it is always resting. In Spring, when the grass is lush, ponies in particular will gorge themselves which can lead to laminitis. Being able to restrict the grazing is therefore useful.

Remove droppings daily especially from small paddocks to help reduce worm infestation. Opinions on the benefits of harrowing the field vary — some believe it to be beneficial while others feel it helps to spread the worm problem. Talk to a local farmer and ask his opinion and advice.

Will my pony need company?

Horses are by nature a herd animal and need company but their grazing mate need not necessarily be of the same species. Although two ponies together can help each other (by standing nose to tail and swishing the flies away) your pony will welcome a cow for instance, just as readily. This can help in other ways too — horses are quite fussy eaters but a cow will graze the areas neglected by the horses and will help to eliminate some of the worm larvae which may have infested the paddock.

How often should I see my pony?

You need to see your horse at least once a day to check that he is still safe and sound and hasn't injured himself. The daily grooming routine for a grass kept animal is explained in chapter 5.

Make a habit of having a regular field maintenance walkabout and if the weather has been particularly windy just check that the fencing and shelter are still secure.

Always keep the water supply in good working order. In winter you will have to make at least two journeys a day to break any ice on the trough or buckets. These visits also give you the chance to check that rugs are still in place.

Putting your feed bucket in an old tyre will ensure that it does not get kicked over and food wasted.

What extra feed will be needed by a grass kept horse?

During summer you may need to give your horse additional hard food — oats, nuts, bran etc. depending on the amount of work he is doing.

In winter you certainly cannot expect your pony to survive without extra food. As the grass loses its feed value (this reduces in July and has gone completely by late autumn) so you must supplement the diet with hay.

Feeding from a rack or haynets tied to the fence or shelter reduces waste and is more economical than feeding hay off the floor. Be careful though that the nets are tied high enough to prevent the horse catching his legs in them.

Give hard feed as necessary, again feeding out of buckets on the floor or mangers which can be hung on the fence or gate.

What problems should I look out for?

All horses need worming but it is generally accepted that it is beneficial to worm grass kept animals more regularly than their stabled counterparts. Every six to eight weeks is advisable, changing the brand of wormer regularly.

If you suspect your horse has worm problems get a worm count done. Your vet will need a sample of the animal's dung which can then be tested. He will advise you on how to deal with the problem.

It's wise to give your pony a thorough dusting over with louse powder at the beginning of the year and in autumn. Most horses and ponies get lice at some time —

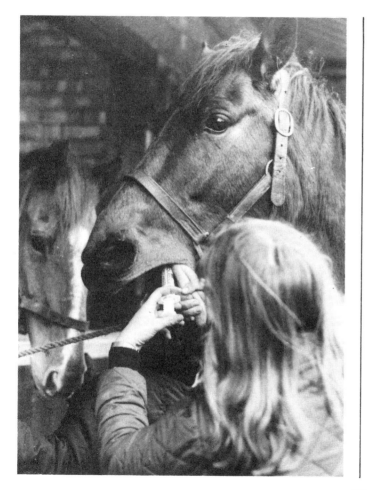

LEFT: *Regular worming is essential for both grass kept and stabled animals.*

ABOVE: *Dusting with louse powder is a sensible precaution.*

they can be found in the pony's thick woolly coat. The powder is available from saddlers and vets — you sprinkle it along the neck and back, rub it well into the coat and repeat the process ten days later.

Sweet itch is quite a common problem which occurs in late Spring/early Summer. It affects the mane and tail areas and the pony may rub himself raw as he tries to relieve the irritation.

If you know your pony suffers from sweet itch the vet will be able to give him some preventative injections earlier in the year before the condition starts. Once the pony begins to suffer from sweet itch injections can be given and benzol benzoate used to ease the soreness.

Warble flies and gadflies lay their eggs on horses in summer. The yellow eggs of the gadflies are within reach of the horses tongue so the larvae are taken into the mouth and later make their way to the stomach where they have an inflammatory effect.

Warble maggots hatch, bore through the skin and appear as small lumps on the horse's back. Here they grow and when mature, break out of the skin to drop to the ground.

Prevention is better than cure. If you see the gadfly eggs clip or scrape them off the horse. Warbles which are not under the saddle area should be left alone to ripen naturally and the maggot can then be squeezed out. Do not use a saddle on a horse with warbles.

Do not try to remove the warble before it is ready otherwise it may burst under the horse's skin and cause infection. Once a warble has been removed wash out the cavity and dress it with wound powder.

What happens if I cannot catch my pony?

When introducing a strange pony in a new field it's best to turn him out in just a small area with his headcollar on. Leave six inches or so of plaited baler twine attached to the headcollar so you have something to catch hold of.

You should have an idea from the previous owner and your trial whether the pony is good to catch or not.

When you go to catch a pony walk up to him quietly keeping the headcollar (if he's not already wearing it) out of sight and talking to him. Approach him to one side so that he can see you and you do not frighten him. Do not get into the habit of rushing up to the pony, hauling him out of the field, slinging on his tack and hurrying out for a ride. This doesn't encourage him to be caught.

There's no harm in giving your pony one titbit when you've caught him. Occasionally just catch him and make a fuss of him before turning him loose again, so he realises that being caught does not always mean work but can be enjoyable.

It is very annoying when a pony will not be caught, but losing your temper will not help.

If there are other ponies in the field and it's feasible, remove them. The offending pony will usually allow himself to be caught if his friends are taken elsewhere.

To catch a pony who is alone and unco-operative try tempting him with food — pony nuts rattling in a bucket can prove too much of a temptation to resist.

Sometimes it's a case of sit down and wait. If you sit quietly in the field curiosity often gets the better of them.

For really difficult ponies you will need help to corner him. Your choice of first pony will have been so knowledgeable that this situation will not arise but even the best behaved can have their silly days.

Laminitis

Laminitis, or fever of the feet, is a very painful

condition, in many cases brought about by too much rich food and insufficient exercise.

The name means inflammation of the laminae — these are at the junction of the pedal bone which forms the centre of the foot and the horny hoof. The process starts with a pony eating too much rich grass — a fatty liver develops and the toxins from the liver affect the blood vessels supplying the sensitive laminae.

As the blood vessels become blocked the blood is forced into the laminae of the foot. The hoof is a firm shape, unable to swell as the pressure builds up so the pony experiences a great deal of pain.

Acute Laminitis

The pony will have a slightly increased temperature and pulse. He may sweat and will puff and blow. He will be reluctant to put any weight on his forefeet and will not want to move. If he does move his gait will be short and shuffling. There will be heat around the coronet and the pony may rock from one foot to another.

Make a point of keeping a close watch on your pony out at grass — the early stages of laminitis can then be detected. Often ponies stand for a long while or lie down flat for much longer than usual. He'll be sluggish to ride and have swelling around the eyes.

You must call the vet immediately — the pony's condition will only worsen without attention. You'll also be saving your pony from a great deal of pain.

Chronic Laminitis

With this the blood leaking into the laminae forces the hoof wall away from the pedal bone. As a result the pedal bone rotates, the sole drops, feet become overgrown and dished and deep ridges appear around the hoof.

Treating Laminitis

Your vet will give injections to help relieve the pain and pressure, and get the liver functioning properly again.

For your part you will have to get the pony's front shoes removed and walk him out. Always follow your vet's instructions — it is not pleasant walking out a pony suffering from this disease but it has to be done.

Cold hosing or standing the pony in a stream will also help to relieve the pain.

For his own sake the pony must be on virtually a starvation diet but with ample drinking water. The skill of your farrier will also be needed to buff the toe right back and level the sides — this helps the rotated pedal bone and dropped sole. The heels will also be taken as low as possible.

Special surgical shoes can be made but they have to be replaced about every three weeks. Broad webbed, they protect the sensitive areas and the full weight is taken by the wall.

Although chronic laminitis cannot be cured completely the sufferers do have the chance of a normal working life. In the future though the owner must keep the pony away from too much rich food and ensure the animal is exercised conscientiously.

Other causes of laminitis include feeding too much corn, an allergy, and, in case of a brood mare, a partially retained afterbirth.

3. STABLED HORSES

An Ideal Home

Most people stable their horses at some time — usually in the winter months — while others may have to keep their horses stabled throughout the year because it is the only option open to them.

When you're looking for a stable bear in mind that

Another form of stalls — as these have solid partitions they offer more protection against biting and bullying. Bedding is usually provided so the horse can lie down and relax — most horses will not stale on to concrete floors so bedding is essential for the horse's wellbeing.

a horse will need a box at least 12ft by 14ft while ponies need 10ft by 12ft. You may be offered accommodation for your horse in the form of stalls — these should be 5ft 6ins wide and 11ft long but bear in mind that your horse will not be able to move around. Often, when stalls are partitioned using swinging bails, there is no protection against bullying or neck-biting.

If you are considering building stables on your own land you need permission first. Even on farms you cannot build stables without planning permission so consult your local authority. Remember that it will take time to get plans drawn up, submitted to the council committee and passed. You may have to make revisions to the plans as well so give yourself plenty of time to sort out the formalities.

When drawing up your plans include a section and elevation of the stable plus details of its position in relation to other buildings. You should also allow room for storing feed, stable equipment and bedding.

Choose a site which is well drained, sheltered from prevailing winds but still with good light, close to water and electricity supplies for convenience.

Sloping roofs are better than flat ones as their design lends itself to good ventilation and plenty of space and light. An overhang reaps benefit in rainy weather as you can still work in the stable area without getting soaked.

A window in a stable is the main inlet for fresh air but you need to protect the horse from the glass by covering with a grid or bars. The window should be situated along the outer wall on the same side as the

Although this box does not look onto a yard it is light and airy — it's also positioned close to a tack room so there is plenty of activity to keep the horse interested.

Stable windows should open with an inward slant with a grid or bars as protection.

door to prevent through draughts and hinged from the bottom edge or the centre so that they may be opened with an inward slant.

The stable floor needs to be as level as possible, with a minimum slope — just enough for drainage. Obviously surfaces should be non-slip, impervious to moisture and hard wearing.

Stable doors should always open outwards in case an animal gets cast (lays down so close to a wall that he cannot get up again) near his door and so that you do not disturb the bedding each time you open the door. Doors should be 8ft high and 4ft wide. Usually the top half is left open to ensure good ventilation, helping to keep horses healthier and less prone to colds.

Latches need to be strong and without any projecting edges which might injure horses. For ease the bottom latch can be foot operated. Always have two latches, one at the top and another at the bottom for extra security — some horses are remarkably adept at undoing bolts! As the top half of the stable door is likely to be open most of the time ensure that it is fastened back and will not bang shut if the wind is strong.

The fewer fittings there are in the stable the better as there is less chance of injury and more room. You will need a couple of tying-up rings — one at breast level, another at eye level. The latter can be used for short

Foot operated bottom latches are labour saving and give extra security.

racking the horses and for haynets but it needs to be about 5ft above the ground.

Mangers should be placed about 3ft 6ins above the ground, with well rounded corners to reduce the risk of injury. A broad, shallow manger is better than a deep narrow one — greedy animals cannot plunge their mouths into the food and grab large mouthfuls. Broad rimmed mangers also discourage the horse from holding the edge and crib biting.

You can get mangers which attach to the door and are removed as soon as the horse has finished. These are also easier to keep clean.

Automatic drinking bowls are a labour saver but always check that they have not become blocked with food — position them away from the manger or hay rack. One disadvantage with automatic supplies is that you cannot tell whether the horse is drinking or not — often one of the early signs if a horse is off colour.

Buckets can be held in rings attached to the stable wall or placed on the floor. However, they need refilling and swilling out several times a day.

Electric light switches should be outside the stable, out of reach of the horse.

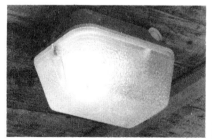

Light fittings should be horse proof.

39

Bedding

Horses need bedding in their stables for the following reasons:

● It helps to prevent injury to the horse.

● A good bed encourages the horse to lie down and relax.

● Bedding will provide warmth around the lower legs and help to prevent draughts.

● Encourages the horse to stale.

● Prevents horse's feet from being jarred by standing on a hard surface for long periods.

● Helps to keep the horse clean and the air pure.

There's now a wide choice of bedding — straw, shavings, peat moss, sawdust and shredded paper. Whichever you choose you must provide enough bedding so that the horse can lie down comfortably, without injuring himself. As an extra precaution against the horse getting cast and injuring himself it is usual to 'bank' the side of the bed (build them up at the edges). This also gives better protection against draughts.

Straw

Old straw is better than new but do not use damp or mouldy bedding. Wheat straw is generally considered to be best as it is easy to obtain and work with, gives a warm bed and a bright appearance to the stable.

Oat straw comes next although horses often eat it. If your horse eats his old bed you can try mixing the new and old bedding together and sprinkling with a disinfectant. This does not deter the most determined in which case you have to think about changing to another material such as shavings.

Providing that it is free from awns barley straw makes quite good bedding but again horses do seem to enjoy eating it.

A quick and easy way of removing droppings from shavings beds.

Shavings

A popular alternative to straw, shavings are readily available packed in bales. Usually economical to use and easy to handle providing you regularly take out droppings throughout the day as well as when you muck out properly.

Sawdust

Can be used on its own or underneath shavings but it should be dry. In some areas it is a cheap source of bedding.

Peat Moss

This does make a good bed but it must be forked and raked daily with wet, soiled patches taken out regularly. It is heavier to work than shavings or sawdust, and sometimes disposing of it is a problem but when rotted it is popular with gardeners.

Shredded Paper

Paper bedding is becoming more popular, especially with the owners of horses who have respiratory problems. Good quality paper bedding, for instance made from packing used in the medical field, has been proved beneficial as it is virtually dust free.

Paper packs down very well, giving a comfy bed which does not displace easily as the horse moves around.

It is also easy enough to handle and can be disposed of simply by burning. Initially it does cost more than straw and shavings but over a long period it proves competitive.

Mucking Out

This job is carried out first thing in the morning when all the wet and soiled bedding is removed, the stable floor is cleaned and aired and a new bed laid.

1. Collect together your equipment — fork, shovel, wheelbarrow, brush, headcollar and rope. If it's a shavings bed some people wear rubber gloves and pick up the droppings. For peat moss beds you'll also need a rake.

2. Either tie up the horse in the stable or turn him out if possible. If the weather's good he could be tied up outside, away from the stable door so there's no chance of him getting tangled up with the wheelbarrow.

3. Remove water and feed buckets. Take out any droppings.

4. Starting at one corner, work systematically through removing soiled bedding. Put dirty bedding into the wheelbarrow and throw clean bedding up against one of the stable walls.

5. Once all the bedding has been sorted, brush the floor thoroughly and if possible leave it to air.

6. If the bed has to be remade straight away mix in any new bedding with the old. Shake up the straw thoroughly and make the bed to a good depth. Test it

by sticking the fork into the bed — if you can hear it clang on the stable floor you need a bit more bedding. Bank up the sides.

7. Sweep the front of the stable and yard, take the dirty bedding to the muck heap.

8. Refill the water buckets and return the horse.

Skipping Out

Throughout the day remove any droppings or wet patches. Keep a plastic laundry basket for this purpose — it's also useful when you pick out the horse's feet as it saves the dirt falling onto a clean bed or yard.

Deep Litter

Some people prefer to give their horses a deep bed and instead of lifting up the entire bed each day they simply remove the soiled bedding and add fresh material as necessary. This takes less time but every three months or so the whole lot has to be removed and a new bed started.

The Muck Heap

Build your muck heap at a convenient spot not too far from the stables but away from anywhere occupied by people as they probably will not appreciate seeing or smelling a manure heap!

Some like to contain the heap within a three-sided brick wall but this is not essential providing you keep the muck heap tidy. After you've mucked out you should see that the latest deposits of manure are packed down tightly. This will help it to rot — you can then sell it as garden fertilizer.

Buying Bedding and Feed

If your horse is at full livery you will not need to worry about buying in hay, bedding materials or feed. For those of you who keep your horse at home or DIY livery you'd be wise to find out where you can get supplies before you actually buy your horse.

You'll see advertisements for local feed merchants in the Yellow Pages or your newspaper. Otherwise ask around other horse owners, saddlers and riding schools. Some saddlers now stock feed and bedding too.

Straw can usually be brought from local farmers — either by the bale or in bulk. It's normally cheaper to buy in quantity but you do need the space to store it. Club together with other horse owners in the same yard and buy in bulk.

Prices vary according to the type of bedding you buy. Straw is normally the cheapest with shavings being, at the time of writing, around £3 a bale and paper £3.50 per bale/sack.

It's best to buy in hay just after it is made rather than wait until winter when stocks start to get low.

Store both hay and straw in a stack, with the bottom layers raised off the ground on wooden pallets so that the bales do not get damp. If you cannot store in a shed or barn then cover the bales with tarpaulin.

You may feed either meadow or seed hay providing it is good quality. Meadow hay is normally slightly cheaper.

There are many varieties of grasses in meadow hay as it is made from permanent pasture. It is slightly green when new but the colour fades with age. The hay should smell sweet and be fairly soft.

Seed hay has a coarser appearance and is made from planted grasses, usually with a high proportion of rye grass.

It is safer not to feed new hay less than six months old as it may be indigestible.

Good hay is free from dust and mould, the grasses are recognisable by their seed heads, it smells sweet and is crisp to the touch.

Through winter you would expect a pony up to 14hh to need approximately one ton of hay and a horse about one and a half to two tons. This is a rough guide, working on 12lbs of hay per day for a pony and 16lbs for a horse. These will vary depending on how much work your horse is doing and the quality of the hay. Generally seed hay has a higher feed value than meadow hay.

Other feedstuffs such as oats do lose their nutritional value if stored for a long while. So while it is not advisable to buy in bulk just for one pony there is no reason why three or four friends could not get together and buy enough to last four ponies for three weeks. You should be able to save a little money this way.

Keeping A Horse At Livery

If you have to pay someone else to look after your horse on their property it is called putting your horse at livery. However, there are different types of livery:

Full:

This is where you pay a set amount per week and everything is done. Additional costs are farrier's and vet's fees, plus worming powders.

You would expect full livery to include: stable, bedding, hay, feed, exercise, grooming and cleaning of tack. Your horse should also be ready for you when you wish to ride.

Everyone's definition of full livery varies so it is worth finding out exactly what is offered.

Naturally you have to pay more for this type of service — around £40 per week for a horse is typical. Any schooling you ask the livery yard owners to do is normally charged extra — as is clipping.

If you are paying for full livery then you should expect your horse to receive adequate food and exercise. If he isn't then speak to the people concerned. Another point worth checking when you make initial enquiries is whether your horse will be turned out at all during the day and how much notice is required before you intend to remove your horse from the yard.

You will be expected to sign a livery agreement at most yards — this authorises them to call out the vet if necessary on your behalf and covers them if they cannot contact you beforehand.

Remember that insurance of tack and horse are your responsibility.

Part livery/Working livery

In these cases you pay part of your horse's keep and the other is made up in kind — ie. the stable has the use of your horse.

This can work well providing you make certain

points clear from the outset. You need to know what standard of rider will be allowed on your horse and how much work he will do, also the times of work as these may conflict with when you want to ride. If he sustains an injury when working as a 'school' animal are they prepared to foot the bill? What happens if the horse is off work for a time — what arrangements will come into force then?

Get all these points in writing so both parties know where they stand. Check the effect on insurance too.

You would not expect to pay more than half the full livery rate for this arrangement. One distinct disadvantage is that if you are preparing for particular competitions your horse's schooling programme may be disrupted by having lots of different riders.

DIY livery

As the name suggests you do the work while paying a fee for the use of the stable and facilities. Some fees are for the stable rent alone, others include use of schooling areas when free etc. Around £7 to £10 for a stable per week would be typical.

Normally you have to supply bedding and food but you may be able to buy hay and straw off the yard owner. Check and compare prices.

This type of livery sounds fine but remember to take into consideration the costs of feed, bedding and extra petrol for twice daily journeys. You may find that it isn't that much cheaper than working livery.

Grass livery

With this type your pony will live out all year although stabling may be available in an emergency.

Around £5-£8 would be expected purely for the grazing. If some short feed and hay was given by the livery yard owners the charge could be £10 per week.

Stable Maintenance

From both the safety and financial aspect it makes sense to look over your stable regularly and carry out necessary maintenance.

Most people choose summer to clean out their stable, give doors a fresh coat of paint and generally tidy up.

Before you do any painting carry out repairs first. Check that the roof is in good order — both inside and out replacing tiles as necessary.

Check the guttering. If it is starting to split replacing it will be cheaper than letting water run down the walls ruining the woodwork.

Replace any broken glass in the windows and check that the catches are not going to give up the ghost. Worn door bolts and hinges should be changed.

Have the electrical wiring checked by a professional and for safety's sake keep fire extinguishers or buckets close at hand and prominently marked. All extinguishers should be regularly serviced in accordance with manufacturer's recommendations.

Give the stable floor and walls a good cleaning with disinfectant, replenish woodwork with another coat of creosote or wood preserver if necessary and repaint where needed.

While you're in the mood, it's worth looking at your stable tools. If they are in good order it will certainly make mucking out easier.

All stabled horses like the chance to relax and let off steam in the field each day.

4. TACK AND EQUIPMENT

After your horse the most expensive items will be your tack and anything else for your horse's wardrobe such as rugs and boots.

Initially though just start with the basics — saddle complete with girth, stirrup leathers and irons, bridle, bit and martingale if used, headcollar, lead rope and grooming kit.

It is not necessary to buy new saddlery but whatever you buy must fit your horse properly, be of good quality and safe. You may see cheap saddles advertised — £50 for a new one but these are usually the inferior quality tack from places such as Pakistan and India. Poorly made tack will soon need attention and most saddlers will not even consider repairing such equipment.

Well made and good quality leather tack costs more to buy initially but you will be repaid by years of service.

A decent pony saddle would cost about £150 upwards whereas a bigger saddle, suitable for horses, could set you back anything from £275 to over £400. If you buy secondhand around £100 should get you a respectable saddle.

Check the advertisements in your local papers and saddlers for details of tack for sale. Most saddles are sold incomplete — i.e. the girth, stirrup irons and leathers have to be bought separately.

If you can buy new tack your saddler ought to be able to visit you with a selection of saddles which you can then try to achieve the best fit for you and your horse.

Types of saddle

A saddle is designed to place the rider's weight over the horse's centre of gravity and to be as comfortable as possible for both horse and rider.

For each equestrian sport the rider's position alters e.g. a forward seat for jumping, so the saddles are made accordingly.

Jumping saddles have more forward cut flaps and good knee rolls to help the rider maintain their forward position while dressage saddles have straight flaps to cater for the rider's longer leg position. As dressage riders need to keep a close contact with their horse the saddle panels are purposely kept free of bulkiness.

Therefore dressage saddles usually have only two girth straps which are much longer than usual, extending below the saddle flap. A much shorter girth is used.

In showing classes where competitors want to show off their pony's shoulder and allow the action to be as free as possible, saddles with straight cut flaps are used.

However most riders use general puspose saddles which are similar in design to jumping saddles but the flaps are not so forward cut.

Structure of a saddle

The framework on which the saddle is built is known as the tree. This used to be made traditionally of beech wood but nowadays laminated wood is popular.

If your saddle is dropped or the horse rolls with the

saddle on his back the tree may be broken. This is serious as a broken tree will injure the horse's back. If you buy secondhand it is wise to get a saddler to check the tree for you before buying.

Should your saddler refuse to help ask your riding instructor for advice or try this simple test yourself. Take hold of the front arch of the saddle with one hand and the centre with the other hand. Now try and bend them towards each other — if there is more than a little give it's possible the tree is broken or damaged. With the modern spring tree saddles there will be some give but if

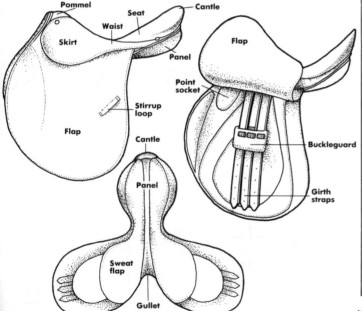

Carrying a saddle easily and safely.

you are doubtful it's worth getting a second opinion.

Saddles may have full or half panels — full ones tend to be more common now. You will note that the stirrup bars to which the stirrups are attached will have a hinged piece on the end. This is a safety catch to be turned up when a horse is being led so that the leathers do not slip off. You should never ride with the hinged piece up — always make sure that it is down: then if you fall off there is less risk of you being dragged along

48

because the whole leather ought to come free of the saddle — imagine the damage if it didn't.

Carrying a saddle

The easiest way to carry your saddle is with the front arch in the crook of the elbow. Your bridle can be carried on the same shoulder so you have the advantage of one hand free to open doors etc. Alternatively you can carry your saddle resting along your thigh, supporting it with your hand in the front arch.

There's bound to be a time when you have to stand the saddle on the floor — it's a valuable piece of equipment so look after it. Stand the saddle on the front arch with the girth folded underneath the pommel to protect the leather from rough ground.

Leather is easily scratched — don't leave the saddle where horses or people can tread on it or knock it over. If you leave it over the stable door while you bridle up, protect it with rugs and watch that your pony doesn't nudge it and send it crashing to the ground.

Fitting a Saddle

A poorly fitting saddle can cause pressure and friction — both of which can hurt the horse. Care when choosing a saddle and keeping it in good order should avoid problems.

● Saddles come in broad, medium and narrow fittings so make sure you get the right one for your horse. The withers should not be pinched by the front arch of the saddle.

● Check that the saddle clears the withers at the front and that there is a clear channel along the backbone. The rider should be able to fit three fingers between the front arch and the withers. Test, when the rider is mounted, that there is still a clear channel between the saddle and the horse's spine.

● The saddle should rest evenly on the horse's back so that the rider's weight is distributed without any undue pressure on either side of the backbone.

● A saddle should be correctly stuffed — if the panels are flat they will cause pressure and soreness as well as restricting the horse's movement. Too much stuffing is as bad as too little for the saddle may rock and rub the horse's back.

● There must not be weight on the loins — a horse's kidneys lie beneath the loins so this weak area should not be subjected to excess strain or weight.

● Have your saddle looked at every year by a saddler who will test the tree, re-stuff if necessary and attend to any worn stitching.

Girths

These are an essential item as they hold the saddle in place! It's wise therefore to check that your girth is always in good order — a girth breaking as you tackle a show jump is an experience you can do without.

There's plenty of choice of materials and type. Leather girths are the best although they do need looking after properly. As you might expect, leather is

the most expensive.

Three fold leather girths are popular — they are made of one piece of leather, folded over twice. You should use them with the folded edge at the front otherwise the horse's skin could be rubbed. These girths have to be kept supple with a strip of material, soaked in neatsfood oil, in the inner fold of the girth.

For horses in soft condition a leather Balding girth is a better choice. These are shaped so they are narrower where the girth fits behind the elbows to avoid rubbing and soreness.

String or nylon girths are good general pupose ones although nylon is harder wearing. Webbing girths are more liable to snap without warning so always use two together.

Lampwick is strong, soft and reasonably priced but it does stretch a little so check its fitting once you've used it a couple of times.

Another good choice is the soft, cotton covered, foam filled girth. These wash easily, are strong and comfortable.

Any girth will rub if you do not remove mud or dirt from your pony's coat where the girth lies. Keep your girth clean too — if your horse sweats and you haven't bothered to wash the sweat out eventually the girth will become hard.

LEFT: A selection of girths, from left to right: string/nylon; Cottage Craft — cotton covered, foam rubber inside; lampwick; leather Balding girth; three fold leather; Atherstone (same principle as Balding girths) and a short dressage girth used with dressage saddles.

Pulling forward the forelegs smooths out any wrinkles of skin in the girth area.

When you do wash a girth (except leather ones) make sure you dry the buckles otherwise they tend to go rusty.

Girths are measured in inches — for example a cobby 15.3hh would probably need a 46 inch or 48 inch girth. To check the fitting the girth should fasten about half way up the girth straps on either side.

When you've tightened your girth make a habit of pulling each of your pony's forelegs forward. Grasp each foreleg in turn just below the knee, pulling the leg forward so the skin under the girth is smooth. This will help to prevent any galling.

Stirrup Leathers

These should be the best quality leather you can afford. With use leather stretches so swop the leathers over now and again otherwise the nearside one, which you use for mounting, will be longer.

As you will tend to use the same holes in the stirrup leather it's a good idea to ask your saddler to shorten them at the buckle end after a good period of use. This will lengthen their life as the wear on the leather will not be restricted to one place.

Stirrup Irons

Stainless steel irons are the best — they look good and are hard wearing. Nickel is too soft and can easily bend or break.

Many irons are sold with integral rubber treads to stop the foot from slipping. If yours do not have them it's worth spending a few extra pence on them.

You should have about half an inch clearance on either side when your foot is in the stirrup — if it's too small your foot could get jammed, too big and your foot may slip through. Either way it could lead to a nasty accident.

Safety stirrups are available for children — they have a thick rubber band as the outside edge of the stirrup instead of metal. The idea is that if the child falls off the band comes undone allowing the foot to come free of the stirrup.

Numnahs

You may wish to use a numnah — a saddle shaped piece of cloth — under the saddle. If the saddle fits well

Numnahs should have about an inch showing all round when it is fitted under the saddle. The front of the numnah should be pulled up into the saddle arch.

there is really no need except that it does help to keep the saddle lining cleaner. If a pony is cold backed or is jumping then you would use a numnah.

They are made of several materials — simulated sheepskin, nylon and cotton covered foam, sheepskin and felt — being attached to the saddle by tapes or loops. You need about one inch of the numnah visible all round when it is fitted under the saddle.

To ensure there is no pressure on the wither or spine pull the numnah up into the front arch before tightening the girth.

Keep the numnah clean — with the woolly types it's important not to allow it to become hard and lumpy as this will rub the horse's back.

Cruppers

Small, barrel like ponies can be difficult to kit out as often the saddle slips forward. This can be remedied by using a crupper — a U-shaped piece of leather with a long leather strap which is fastened on to the D ring at the back of the saddle.

The U-shaped part of the crupper fits under the pony's dock so it must be kept well oiled and supple or it will chafe. Fit the crupper so that it sits comfortably — you do not want it pulling on the tail.

Fitting a crupper so that it lies comfortably without pulling on the horse's tail.

Breastplates

When riding across country, perhaps jumping down drops or going up hill, your saddle may slip back. To prevent this a breastplate can be used.

Hunting type breastplates are commonly seen — they consist of a neck strap which is attached to the front D rings of the saddle on either side of the withers. Another piece of leather goes between the horse's forelegs and is attached to the girth.

An Aintree type breastplace has a web or elastic strap which fits across the breast and attaches to the girth straps under the saddle flaps.

A leather strap across the neck in front of the withers then holds the breast strap in position.

Wither Pads

These should only be used in an emergency to prevent pressure from the front arch of the saddle on the withers. A woollen cloth is folded and placed under the front arch but you should have the saddle re-stuffed or change it rather than run the risk of a poorly fitting saddle causing injury.

Bridles

If you buy a bridle new you will get the headpiece, browband, two cheek pieces, cavesson noseband and reins. The bit has to be bought separately.

Like headcollars bridles come in pony, cob and full size and should be fitted properly on your horse.

It pays to have good quality leather but new leather

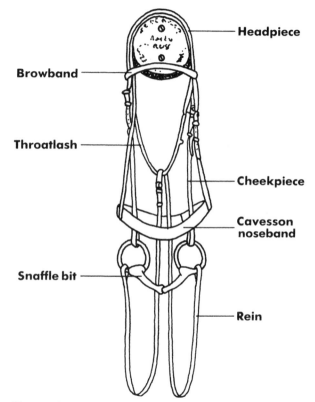

will stretch so you may have to adjust the fitting after a while.

Webbing bridles are now available and although still comparatively new, they are strong, smart and easy to keep clean.

Fitting:

● The throatlash should never be tight — you ought to be able to put the full width of your hand between it and the side of the jaw bone.

● Your pony will feel most uncomfortable if his browband is too tight and pinching his ears. It should lie below them, not touching the ears and long enough to lie comfortably without interfering with the way the head-piece hangs.

● A cavesson noseband should be half way between the projecting cheekbone and the corners of the mouth. You should be able to get two fingers between the horse's nose and the noseband.

● If you use a dropped noseband instead of a cavesson it must be carefully fitted. The front needs to be well above the nostrils so that it does not interfere with the air flow while the back sits in the chin groove. It should be tight enough to stop the horse crossing his jaw.

● The bit needs to be the correct width for the horse's mouth. To check hold the bit with a hand on either side so that the joint is straight. When it is in the horse's mouth it should protrude about a quarter of an inch each side and should be fitted so that it just crinkles the corners of the horse's mouth.
    If you fit the bit too low it can bang on the horse's teeth or he may get his tongue over it — too high and his

LEFT: A correctly fitted drop noseband.

mouth will look stretched and he will be uncomfortable.

● Do not use rough edged bits — they will only hurt your pony.

Nosebands

A cavesson noseband is used to complete a bridle and as the attachment for a standing martingale. It is the only type of noseband which does not complement the action of the bit.

Drop nosebands are meant to keep the horse's mouth shut while pressure is applied on the bit.

If you need to use a standing martingale and your horse is normally ridden in a drop noseband then you will have to change his noseband to a flash. The upper part of this noseband is like a cavesson so you can attach the standing martingale to it, but it has a lower part which acts like a drop.

The Grackle or cross noseband is useful on very strong horses as it prevents them from crossing their jaw. The point of pressure is where the straps intersect. The straps fasten above and below the bit and you must be careful that the top ones do not rub the cheekbones and the lower ones do not interfere with the horse's breathing.

Martingales

These are artificial schooling aids which are often abused. In a perfect world your horse would go happily on the bit with a relaxed back, flexed neck and working properly through from his quarters. A martingale properly fitted will not interfere with the horse when he's

going well but should anything untoward happen it will come into effect.

Imagine your horse suddenly flinging his head up as you came into a jump. The effect would be a stiff, hollow back, a flat jump and probably one which resulted in the horse hitting the fence. In these

A running martingale, fitted properly, does not interfere with the horse — it only comes into action when the horse flings his head up too high.

circumstances a properly fitting martingale would help the rider to lower the horse's head and stop any evasion of the bit.

Running Martingales

These consist of a neck strap, and a piece of leather which goes between the horse's frontlegs to the girth. At the other end the strap divides into two, with rings on each end through which the reins pass.

Correctly fitted the front straps should be long enough to reach upwards level with the withers. If too tight there will be a constant downward pressure on the bit — too loose it's a waste of time and could be dangerous.

Always use rein stops to prevent the martingale rings catching on the rein fastenings.

Standing Martingales

With these the pressure is on the nose rather than the mouth so it's a good choice on a young horse when extra control is needed.

Standing martingales have a leather strap with a loop on one end which fits on to the back of the cavesson noseband. The other end attaches to the girth and there is the usual neckstrap.

Fitted properly there should be enough front strap to hold up into the horse's jaw. If it's too tight it will stop the horse from stretching his neck.

Neckstraps on martingales should be fitted with the buckles on the nearside.

Reins

There are various types of reins — rubber, plaited,

Standing martingales need careful fitting too or you could restrict the head movement.

plain, nylon.

Rubber reins are ideal for riding in wet conditions as you still have some grip whereas plain leather can become too slippery.

At one time coloured nylon type reins were popular especially with children but they do stretch and slip.

Bits

Ideally a first pony or horse should be happy in an ordinary snaffle bridle although if you are hunting or riding across country you may need a stronger bit for extra control.

There are a whole host of bits used for various reasons. Some riders always seem to be changing their horse's bit which makes you wonder whether it would be better for them to look at their riding ability and the horse's basic schooling rather than changing the metalwork.

Remember that you do not control your horse simply by using your hands — the other aids, your legs, seat and body are all used too.

Through the bit we apply pressure to the horse's mouth, he relaxes his jaw so giving way to the pressure and we thank him by yielding. You cannot make the horse do anything — you must ask him. In a battle of strength the horse will always win.

When a horse is first ridden his introductory bit is a snaffle. The purpose is to teach him to accept the bit with a supple jaw, a still and correct head. If the horse goes well in this he can be ridden in it for the rest of his life unless circumstances dictate otherwise — for example the horse may be trained up to advanced level dressage in which case he will be trained to go in a double bridle so that more refined aids can be used.

There are four main bitting families:

Snaffle: from the word meaning to make or break, has one bit, one rein and is the simplest, most common form.

Double Bridle: has two sets of reins, two bits and is used by more experienced riders.

Pelham: one bit but two sets of reins when used correctly. May be adapted to use just one set of reins but this makes the action of the bit vague.

Bitless Bridle: one rein and relies on pressure on the nose for control.

There are seven control points and the various bits will act on one or more of these points:

1. Bars of the mouth — i.e. the gum between the incisors, and the molars. The bars are sensitive and can easily be damaged.

2. Lips/corners of the mouth

3. Tongue

4. Nose

5. Poll

6. Roof of the mouth

7. Chin or curb groove — the groove under the pony's chin where the curb chain lies.

Snaffles

These bits act on the lips and corners of the mouth,

A French bridoon.

the tongue and the bars. In its simplest form the snaffle has a head raising action.

You may have an unjointed, jointed or double jointed snaffle. Young horses are started in straight bar or mullen mouth snaffles — these are unjointed but the latter has a slight curve on the mouthpiece. They are usually made of rubber or vulcanite when the horse first has a bit in his mouth.

Some horses lean on this bit or get their tongue over in which case you can try a jointed snaffle. These have a squeezing or nutcracker action on the tongue and lower jaw — this will be increased if the joint is loose and worn, making your pony uncomfortable in his mouth.

With any bit it is important they are in good condition and fit your horse otherwise he will not be happy in his mouth and therefore unable to concentrate on his job.

Snaffles with fixed sides have less 'play' in them than the loose ringed ones but they prevent any pinching on the corners of the pony's mouth. You can try a bit with

cheeks if you pony has a habit of opening his mouth as you turn.

Some animals are rather fussy in their mouths and will not accept the nutcracker action of a jointed snaffle. To break up this action the French bridoon has a centre link which lies flat on the pony's tongue — it is a fairly mild bit.

Another bit with a link is the Dr. Bristol but this is quite different in its action to the French bridoon. The plate is set at an angle so that it puts pressure on the tongue and is therefore useful with stronger ponies.

Pelhams

The other bitting family less experienced riders are likely to come across is the Pelham. As this bit tries to combine the best of the snaffle and the double bridle its action is rather vague. Yet strangely enough some ponies go far better in a Pelham than anything else.

Used correctly it has two reins, the top or snaffle rein on the outside of the curb rein. The snaffle rein has a head raising action, the curb lowers the head.

As it has two reins which some children find difficult to cope with a rounding is attached to convert the bit for one rein. The rounding is supposed to be such that the rein can rise to the top to act as a snaffle rein and slip down as the rider lowers their hands to give a curb effect. To achieve this you must keep the rounding clean and well-oiled and be well aware of its action.

Always think about riding your horse forward and beware of letting your hands become heavy or wooden.

A pelham has a curb chain which applies downward pressure on the lower jaw when the curb is in action. A stainless steel, double linked curb chain is best

as single link chains are not as comfortable. You can buy rubber guards to fit over the chain and protect the horse's chin groove.

When you use a curb chain you should clip the hair in the chin groove to allow air to circulate. Wash the area after you've ridden to prevent sores.

To fit a curb chain, fasten it onto the righthand hook and pass it under the horse's chin. Stand on the lefthand side and twist the whole chain clockwise so all the links lie flat against each other. The chain can then be attached to the nearside hook but do not fit it too tightly.

A member of the pelham family which is useful as a 'change' bit is a Kimblewick or Spanish jumping bit. It has one rein and a curb chain and riders should appreciate how the position of their hands affects the action of the bit. By raising the hands the bit has a snaffle action, by lowering them the rein slips down and in conjunction with the curb chain has a curb effect.

If you do use this bit, perhaps for cross country or hunting, it's important that you do not ride with low hands all the time or the curb will continually be in action.

Caring for tack

As tack takes quite a large chunk out of your savings it is well worth looking after it properly. Not only will this ensure longer service but it gives you the chance

LEFT: Pelham bits ought to be used with two reins or the action of the bit is rather vague.

to carry out a safety check. Any buckles or stitching which need attention should be repaired or replaced immediately.

Ideally tack should be cleaned every time it is used but this is not always practical. Try to give your tack a quick wipe over each time you finish riding and as you do so look out for any weak spots where stitching is coming apart or leather splitting.

If time is short leave your thorough tack cleaning to the weekend, then take your saddle and bridle to pieces and give it the 'works.'

As you take the bridle to bits the first few times take careful note of which holes everything fits in to — then you won't have to keep fitting the bridle.

With all leatherwork use a damp sponge and tepid, not hot, water to remove mud, dirt and grease. If you have trouble getting the grease off use some hair from your horse's tail, rolled into a ball.

Make sure you clean the underside of your bridle and saddle too. Wash the bit and stirrup irons in water and dry them with a soft cloth. Brush any mud off your girth using an old dandy brush — if necessary wash the girth.

Once everything is clean use a slightly damp sponge to apply the saddle soap. You do not want any lather on your leather so do not make the sponge too moist. Use a circular movement as you soap the saddle — panel, girth straps, sweat flap, seat, both sides of the saddle flap and skirt. Soap the stirrup leathers, girth guards and the girth if leather.

RIGHT: Horse hair rolled into a ball is good for removing grease from saddles.

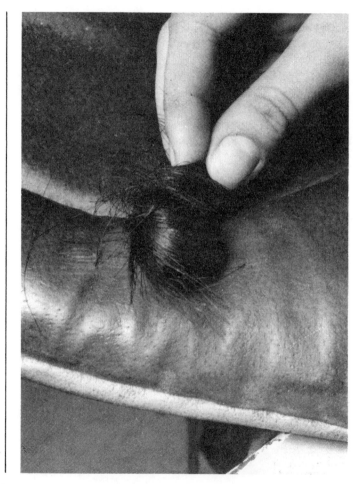

Now to the dismantled bridle. It is usually easier if you have a hook suspended from the ceiling to hang the pieces of the bridle from. Soap everything well taking particular care to attend to the folds in the leather as these are the first to show signs of cracking. Check all buckles and studs are sound and make sure no soap is left in the bridle holes.

Reassemble your sadldle and bridle. To 'put up' a bridle loop the reins through the throastlash and fasten the throatlash: put the cavesson noseband around the whole bridle and fasten it. If your girth is leather do not leave it attached to one side and folded over the saddle. Always take your girth off completely and lay it over the saddle.

Regular cleaning should keep your tack supple and therefore much more comfortable for you and your horse. Dirty tack can gall a pony so leading to time off work.

Once or twice a year you can use a leather dressing on all your tack — boots and rug fastenings as well as saddle and bridle. Use these oils sparingly as they penetrate the leather well and waterproof it.

If you intend to store any saddlery for a while — perhaps because your pony is unfortunately off work, apply a thin layer of vaseline or neatsfoot oil to keep the leather pliable.

With your horse's boots brush off any mud or grit — left on this can rub his legs. Keep the straps well oiled as neglected straps are very difficult to do up. Saddle soap all the leather regularly. With over reach boots scrub them clean and dry away from direct heat.

Never keep your tack in a very warm, dry or damp atmosphere.

Rugs

Choosing a rug for your horse can be bewildering — there's such a range of materials and qualities.

If your horse is going to be clipped during winter you'll need a stable rug and probably extra blankets together with a roller unless the rug has its own integral surcingles. Waterproof New Zealand rugs are a must if your pony is living out all winter and they are also used for stabled horses who are turned out to grass for some time during the day.

Let's take a look at the various rug types and some of the features to look for:

Day Rug — usually woollen or woollen mix and bound with braid. Used as a stable rug during the day or as a rug to keep the chill off at a show. The owner's initials may be sewn on the side.

Night Rug — used for warmth in the stable at night. Made of jute or quilted material.

Most people make do with one stable rug which is worn both night and day. It's handy to have a spare rug in case one needs repairing but with costs to watch there's little point in having a smart day rug simply so your horse looks better in the day.

The choice of stable rugs is now superb. Traditionally stable rugs were jute lined with a wollen material, but now there is a range of quilted rugs of all types of quality. You can spend less and buy a thinner quilted rug but some of the top range are well worth the extra. If they are high quality, well made and well looked after they will give good service.

When choosing a rug try it on your horse as some are better shaped than others. Make sure there is sufficient depth to keep him warm, the lining will be warm, and that any attached surcingles are sensibly positioned avoiding pressure on the spine. There should be enough room round the shoulders to prevent rubbing. You can always sew sheepskin pads on to rugs if they do chafe anywhere.

Check that the fastenings are good quality and easy to deal with. A rug which has an overlap and double fastenings at the chest is preferable to one which leaves a large gap at the front.

Woollen blankets — these are used under rugs to give extra warmth to clipped horses. You do not have to buy proper horse blankets — try picking up some blankets in bedding sales. These are usually perfectly adequate and much cheaper.

Roller — for some rugs (and when you use blankets) you need a roller to secure it all. They are padded so that they avoid pressure directly on the spine. Most owners use a piece of foam rubber under the roller as extra protection.

When putting on a blanket have it well forward on the neck and then fold back the front corners so they lie neatly on the neck. The rug is placed on top and the triangle made by the blankets folded back over the front of the rug. The roller is put on over this to secure the blankets and rug.

New Zealand rugs — made of waterproof canvas and lined either fully or partially with woollen or woollen mix material. The weight of canvas can vary so buy the best you can afford.

The legstraps on a New Zealand may chafe the horse if they are too thin although strap covers can be bought or made. Leather straps and fastenings will last longer, if oiled occasionally.

The better New Zealands are shaped around the quarters to give extra protection against the elements. Some rugs stay in place or right themselves, others have surcingles attached. Again try to avoid any pressure on the spine.

Anti-sweat rugs — made of open cotton mesh, better quality ones feel heavier than economy rugs. They are used to help cool the horse, and with straw underneath to help dry a horse off.

Summer Sheets — made of light cotton, either in checked materials or one colour bound with contrasting tape. They help protect a groomed horse against dust and flies. A fillet string attached to each side of the rug and goes underneath the tail helps to stop the sheet blowing in the wind.

Care

Keep all rugs clean and well aired. Soap the leather parts regularly. When clothing isn't needed for a while wash it, repair it if necessary and then put into store.

A well cut New Zealand, with plenty of depth, which fits well and offers good protection against the elements.

Fitting

The arrival of winter means that rugs are bought and deposited on horses. However the rug must fit properly if it is to do the job well — New Zealand rugs which are too short, stable rugs which rub the shoulders and so on can easily be avoided.

First you need to know what size of rug to even try on your horse. Generally rug sizes are in feet and inches.

The usual method is to measure from the centre of the horse's chest, around his shoulder along his side to an imaginary vertical line drawn down from the horse's dock.

Some makes of rug however are measured from the start of the horse's withers to the root of his tail. It's best to take both sets of measurements and a depth measurement too — from the withers to about four inches down the leg. Cheaper rugs may be short of depth so it's beneficial to shop around and find a manufacturer who specialises in a generous cut.

Armed with your figures you can visit a saddlers or look around the trade stands at shows. What you buy depends on your budget but it is usually more economical in the long term to buy a decent, more expensive but well made rug which will last, than a cheap, poor quality one which may not even survive one winter.

Most saddlers will let you exchange the rug if it does not fit too well — providing of course that it is returned in a clean condition.

Do not just fling a rug over your pony's back — he may object. Put safety first — even ponies used to rugs may be nervous of a new one which rustles.

● Fold the rug into three with the neck and breast fastenings as the top fold. Place the folded rug on the withers.

● Bring forward the neck section and fasten the buckles.

● Pull the rear of the rug towards the tail, sliding the rug

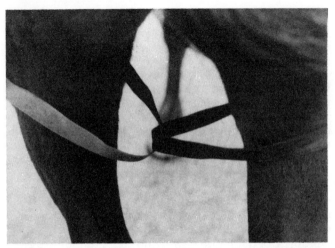

Hind leg straps on rugs should be interlocked and fitted to allow a hand's width between the horse's thigh and strap.

into position, using both hands and standing level with the horse's hip. The horse's coat should lie smooth.

● Take the left leg strap, pass it between the hind legs and fasten it to the left side. Take the right leg trap and repeat the process but linking it through the other strap. There should be enough room to fit the width of your hand between the leg strap and the horse's thigh.

Many New Zealand rugs now do not have surcingles as they are self righting. If the rug you are using has a roller then put on the rug, smooth it into

position and fasten the roller before fastening the chest buckles or leg straps. This ensures that if the pony is frightened and breaks loose he will not be made worse by a rug hanging round his legs or underneath him. Before the roller is on the rug will fall off completely if the horse leaps about.

Protecting Your Horse

When you start competing you're likely to want to protect your horse against injury using boots or bandages. If schooling your horse it's sensible to take the extra few minutes to fit boots just in case he does knock himself over a jump.

Overreach Boots

Used to: protect the horse from over reach wounds. Worn on front feet.
Fitting: They are made of bell shaped rubber which should be turned inside out and pulled over the foot upside down. Once on they can be turned the right way up. Some have fastenings at the side to save you the effort of pulling them on but this type tend to come off easier as you are jumping or galloping across country.

Also useful for a horse which tends to tread on itself when travelling.

Brushing Boots

Used to: protect the fetlock area from brushing wounds. Are always used if you lunge a horse.
Fitting: The longer boots are worn on the hind legs,

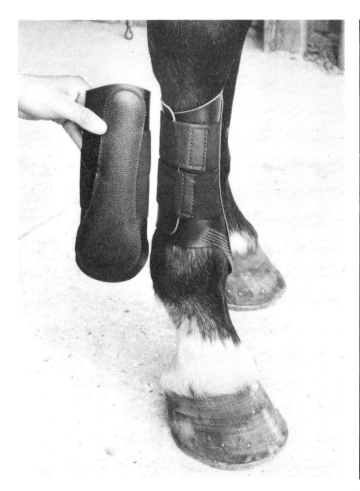

shorter ones on the forelegs. Usually have three, four or five straps. The straps should always point backwards and the boot fitted so that the straps are on the outside.

Place the boot slightly above the area you want to cover and slide it into place so that the hair lies smooth. Fasten the middle or second highest strap first and keep the pressure even all the way along the boot.

When you undo any boot give the leg a quick rub over where the boot or bandage has been.

Yorkshire Boots

Used to: protect against brushing wounds — a cheaper form of boot made of felt.
Fitting: They are normally used on the hind legs. These boots are made of a piece of oblong felt with a tape sewn across it. With the high side pointing upwards the tapes are tied around the leg above the fetlock joint. The top section of felt is then folded down to give extra protection.

Skeleton Knee Caps

Used to: protect a horse from broken knees if he slips on a road — a sensible precaution when hacking out in winter. Also good for young horses when you are schooling them over fixed fences.
Fitting: The top strap needs to be tight enough to stop the knee cap from falling down. Keep the lower strap loose to allow freedom of movement. This strap stops the boot flapping around.

LEFT: Brushing boots protect the fetlock area.

Tendon Boots

Used to: give protection and support to the tendons. Sometimes a horse may strike into himself higher than with a normal over-reach and may catch the tendon.

Fitting: Usually have three, four or five straps, with the boots fitted in much the same way as brushing boots. With these boots the bulkiest part is around the back to protect the tendon rather than at the side to protect the fetlock.

Exercise Bandages

Used to: protect and support the legs during exercise, fast work, jumping and as a substitute for brushing boots.

Fitting: bandages are made of elasticated material and should be used over gamgee or similar material so that the pressure is evened out.

Wrap the gamgee around the leg keeping it smooth and flat. Start bandaging just below the knee leaving a section of the bandage as an overlap. Make one turn around the leg and then bring down the overlap. Bandage down the leg to the fetlock joint and then back up. Finish by tying the tapes on the outside of the leg — not on the bone at the front or tendon at the back.

Tuck the ends of the tapes in and for extra security when competing sew the tapes and then put sticky tape on top. A bandage coming undone as you fly across country can be a real problem.

Be careful that you have even pressure all the way down the bandage. It should not be too tight — you ought to be able to slip a finger between the bandage and leg.

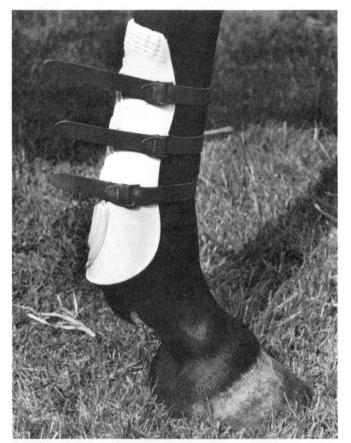

Tendon boots — the straps on boots always point backwards.

Do not use these bandages without padding underneath.

Stable Bandages

These are made of flannel or wool and are used in the stable for warmth, with straw underneath to help dry wet legs, and as protection when travelling.

For warmth or travelling use them over gamgee or some other padding.

Tail Bandage

Helps to protect the tail from injury or rubbing during travelling, and is used to improve the appearance of the tail. The bandage is made of stockinette or crepe, two and a half to three inches wide.

Never leave a tail bandage on for long periods — certainly not all night.

To put on the bandage damp the tail. You should never damp the bandage as it could shrink as it dries and injure the tail.

Unroll about four inches of bandage and place this under the tail, holding the end in the left hand. Make a turn to secure the bandage and then fold the spare bandage down. Carry on bandaging, keeping even pressure and spacing between each turn. Finish just above the end of the tail bone, secure tapes but fairly loosely and bend the tail gently back into position.

When you take the tail bandage off grasp it firmly near the root of the tail and slide it downwards. The only time you unwrap a tail bandage to remove it is when you have applied a bandage over a plaited tail.

General Rules for Bandaging

● Do not draw any part of the bandage tighter than another as uneven pressure can cause serious damage eg. to the tendons in the legs.

● If you draw the tapes tighter than the bandages you'll cause a swelling and possibly even a permanent lump on the leg.

● Tie tapes on the inside or outside of the leg, never on the tendons or bone. Do not use a pin to secure the tapes.

● Do not leave bandages on for long periods — take them off and then replace them if necessary.

● When bandaging swollen legs use plenty of padding underneath and bandage loosely.

● Do not kneel down near a horse's leg to bandage him. For safety's sake bend or crouch down.

● As you are removing stable/exercise bandages unwind them quickly passing the bandage from hand to hand. Do not try to roll them up again at the same time.

● Let bandages dry and air before rolling them up ready for use again.

● Roll them up with the tapes folded inwards.

5. GROOMING

Grooming is the attention we give to the horse's coat and feet each day. One of the most obvious reasons for this is to make the pony look better but the benefits go much further than this.

Daily grooming stimulates the horse's circulation, improves muscle tone and keeps the animal clean so helping to prevent disease.

To groom or 'strap' a horse properly takes 30-45 minutes and is best done after exercise when the horse's skin is warm, his pores are open and the scurf has risen to the surface.

You'll need a headcollar and rope plus your grooming kit which should consist of:

Dandy brush: used to remove mud and caked on dirt. Especially useful if your horse is grass kept. Don't use this brush on the mane or tail as it will split or remove the hairs.

Body Brush: has shorter, softer bristles than the dandy brush, used to remove dirt, scurf and grease from the coat. Also used on the mane and tail.

Curry comb: may be made of metal or rubber. Used to clean the body brush although rubber ones are also used for getting mud off heavy-coated animals. They should be used gently in small circles but not on any bony parts such as the head and lower legs.

Hoof pick: to remove dirt from the underside of the hoof.

Hoof oil & brush: oil applied to walls and underside of hooves to replace lost natural oils and also for improved appearance.

Sponges: use separate ones to clean out the eyes, nostrils and dock.

Water brush: used damp to lay the mane, remove stable stains and clean feet.

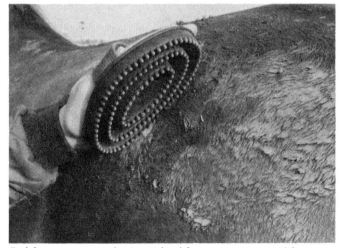
Rubber curry combs are ideal for removing mud from a pony's coat.

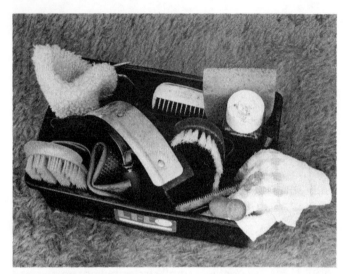

A typical grooming kit containing hoof pick, mane comb, sponge, hoof oil and brush, curry combs, sweat scraper, body brush and stable rubber. Dandy and water brushes are normally included too.

Mane and tail comb: may be metal or plastic, for removing tangles in the hair but generally for pulling the mane or tail.

Wisp: can be leather pad or made of hay — helps to stimulate circulation, to develop and harden muscles.

Stable rubber: cloth used to give horse final wipe over at end of grooming.

How to Groom

1. Collect together your kit, headcollar and rope. Tie the horse up — outside if the weather is good. Remove any rugs.

2. Pick out the feet, always using the pick from the heel to the toe to prevent injuring the soft parts of the frog. An old dandy brush is great for ensuring that the foot is really clean.

Check that the shoes are in good order and the foot is not showing any signs of problems such as thrush.

3. Using a damp water brush remove any stable stains.

4. Starting at the poll region on the near side work all over the body, using a body brush. You should lean your weight behind each stroke of the brush, using short circular movements in the direction of the coat.

The shorter bristles of this brush penetrate the coat to the skin beneath. After four or five strokes clean the brush by drawing the curry comb across it and tapping out the dirt on the floor.

5. Now attend to the mane and tail. You may have to separate tangles using your fingers or a comb. If your pony has a fine mane and tail it's better to gently separate the hair using your fingers. Brush out a few locks of hair at a time using the body brush.

With the mane make sure you throw it over the other side of the neck and brush the crest thoroughly.

When you are doing the mane you can brush the head too. Remove the headcollar and tie it around the

When picking out the feet use the pick from heel to toe.

horse's neck. Use one hand to steady the head and brush carefully with the other, taking extra care in the eye region. Replace the headcollar properly as soon as you have finished.

6. You can now wisp the horse to help develop and harden muscles. Bring the wisp down with a bang in the direction of the coat on the sides of the neck, quarters and thighs. Don't wisp on the loin region which is a tender area or any bony parts.

Wisping also helps to produce a shiny coat and to improve the blood supply by stimulating the skin.

7. Using a damp sponge carefully wipe around the eyes, working from the corners and then around the eyelids. Wring out the sponge and then attend to the muzzle dealing with the lips, inside and outside the nostrils.

With a second damp sponge cleanse the dock, lifting up the tail and sponging the underside of the tail too.

8. Lay the mane by smoothing it down with a damp water brush, working from the mane roots downwards.

9. You can wash the feet providing the weather is not too cold. Use the water brush and keep your thumb pressed into the horse's heel to stop water becoming lodged there. When the hooves are dry you can put hoof oil on the sole, frog, heels and wall.

10. Before replacing any rugs wipe over the horse with a damp stable rubber.

Grass kept ponies

With these you'll find your dandy brush is used more than the body brush as there will be more dirt and mud to remove. In winter don't go overboard with the grooming as your pony needs the natural oils in his coat to protect him against the rain and cold.

Quartering and Setting Fair

These terms are used to describe the quick brush over given to horses before exercising and at evening stables.

Quartering involves removing the stable stains, picking out the feet, sponging eyes, nose and dock, generally making the horse tidy before you ride.

In the evening pick out the feet and brush the horse over lightly before putting on any rugs.

Don't forget

It's safer to bend or squat down to attend to the horse's legs rather than kneel on the floor. When you're brushing the hind legs you can hold the tail in your free hand to discourage the horse from kicking.

Keep your grooming kit clean by regularly washing all the brushes.

Bathing your horse

During hot weather your horse may be sweaty after a ride and will enjoy a bath. If you are competing regularly, especially in show classes, you will want him to look really clean.

However, you must pick your day carefully as horses are susceptible to chills. Always make sure you dry him thoroughly too.

You'll need plenty of warm water, horse shampoo, sponges, sweat scrapers and towels.

First of all wet the horse's body except for his head which is left until last. Apply the shampoo, either by hand or with a sponge, rubbing it in so you get a lather.

ABOVE: Be careful around your pony's eyes whenever you bath or groom him. RIGHT: Swirling the tail round after you've washed it helps to dislodge any remaining water.

72

Then rinse off throughly — you'll probably need to do this two or three times until you're sure you've got rid of all the shampoo. Use a sweatscraper to remove any surplus water but don't use this below the knees or hocks.

With a damp sponge clean the head and lower legs. To wash the tail wet it and then rub in the shampoo. Rinse it well, immersing the tail in a bucket of water. Squeeze the water out gently and then swing the tail round to remove any remaining water. Carefully brush the tail out and apply a clean, dry tail bandage.

Rub the horse's body as dry as possible, taking extra care with the legs and heels. If you have chosen the right day you should be able to walk your horse dry in the sunshine. When he is dry you can brush him over with a clean body brush.

Pulling and Plaiting

Your horse will look much better if his mane and tail are kept tidy and not allowed to become too long.

If you have a native breed or an Arab you can leave their manes and tails 'natural' — not pulled or plaited. These animals are shown natural if they are pure bred.

Pulling

This is used to shorten and thin out the mane. Using a mane comb you select a few of the long hairs from underneath the mane, wind them round the comb and pull them out briskly. Do this working your way up the mane, removing a few hairs at a time.

Some horses object to this so you may have to spread the pulling over several days. Always pull the mane after exercise as the pores are open and the hair comes out easier. Don't pull any top hairs and never use scissors or clippers on the mane.

You can also pull the tail, especially if you want to show off your pony's quarters or make the tail look better. If your pony lives out leave him with a full tail as he will need it for protection against the weather.

To pull a tail remove a few hairs at a time, starting underneath the dock and working sideways, taking care to pull evenly on each side of the tail.

The tail should be level with the pony's hocks — if it's too long ask a friend to put their arm beneath the root of the tail while you cut off the end until it is at the right level.

Plaiting

To give your pony a really smart appearance for a competition plait his mane. This will show off his neck and crest and plaiting helps to train the mane to fall on the correct side (the offside) of the neck.

You'll have to pull his mane first so it is a reasonable length for plaiting. Dampen the mane and divide it into equal sections — you should have an even number of plaits including the forelock.

Start at the top of the mane. Usually the width of the mane comb determines the right amount of plait unless your horse has a very thick mane in which case three-quarters of the length of a comb can be used. Keep the mane which is not being plaited out of the way by pushing it back with the comb.

Divide your section of mane into three and plait

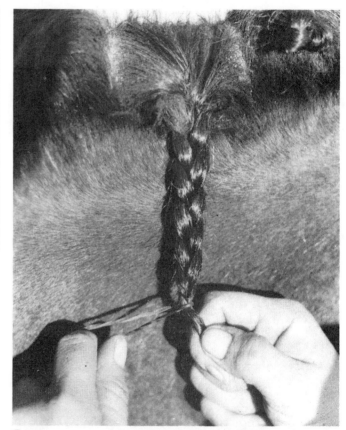

For neatness use thread to plait with but for quickness you can use rubber bands — these would suffice for hunter trial classes but for showing you'd use thread.

74

firmly down to the end of the hair. This can now be secured with thread or rubber bands. The plait is then looped under again, secured and folded for the final time. It should form a neat, tight ball which has to be firmly secured.

To plait a tail you need one that is tangle free. The tail should not have been pulled or rubbed. Start by damping the tail, taking a few hairs from either side of the tail at the top, and sewing them together so you have a piece of hair to work with.

Take a few strands of hair from each side and pass them beneath and across one another instead of passing them over the top as you do with normal plaiting.

Continue plaiting down the tail, feeding in strands of hair from each side until you are within an inch of the bottom of the dock. Then plait the remaining strands down the centre of the tail, wind thread around the bottom of the plait to secure the end and tuck it under.

Stitch down the plait to keep it secure and neat and then straighten the lines of each plait to keep it looking tidy.

Clipping

As winter approaches it's time to start thinking about clipping your pony. This means removing some or all of his winter coat so that he can work without sweating up easily. However, as you are taking away his natural method of keeping warm you must rug him up so that he does not suffer.

If you plan only to ride at weekends and then just gently hacking it will not be worth clipping. Regular

work, including competitions and hunting, will mean clipping is worthwhile.

In winter horses grow thicker coats to protect them against the cold. If you then work the horse hard and fast

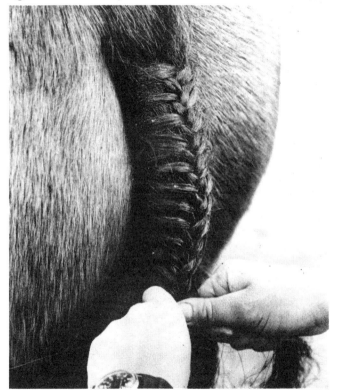

Tail plaiting is an art you can practice.

75

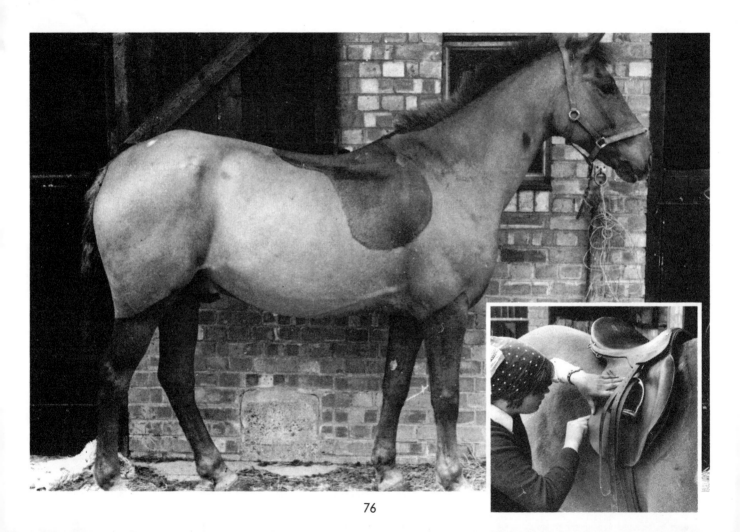

(eg. a show jumping or cross country competition) the horse will sweat heavily. Long, thick coats take time to dry off so there is the risk of the horse catching a chill.

So if your horse is working it is to his benefit to be clipped. It's easier to keep a clipped pony clean than it is to argue with thick, muddy winter coats.

Ponies with native blood will have thicker coats than more quality animals. Usually by mid-October the winter coat has 'set' and you can think about clipping.

By October advertisements start to appear in local newspapers giving details of people who will clip a pony for you. The cost varies according to the type of clip but about £18 for a full clip on a horse would be typical. Clipping services are also advertised on the notice boards of local saddlers. If your pony is in livery at a private yard or riding school they will probably offer this service too.

You may decide to do your own clipping and one way of learning this art is by practising on your own horse. For the first time though you should ask someone who has clipped before to help you, otherwise you could end up with a very odd looking horse!

To buy a pair of clippers will set you back around £100 to £140. Occasionally you see secondhand ones for sale.

It's likely that your horse will need clipping more than once during the winter so you have to decide whether it's better to buy your own or pay someone else each time he needs clipping.

Assuming that you are going to clip your own horse you have to decide how much of his coat you are going to remove.

Types of Clip

There are a number of clips, each 'designed' for the amount of work the pony will be doing. The harder the work, the more coat you remove.

A full clip is the easiest to do because every hair comes off — from the body, head and legs. You do not even leave a patch of hair where the saddle fits.

This would only be needed if the animal was working hard throughout the week — perhaps a couple of days hunting or competing regularly.

If you do give a horse a full clip he will need to live in, have rugs and blankets on and be kept on the move when out of the stable. If the weather is bad it may be necessary to use an exercise sheet when riding out.

Another suitable alternative for stabled ponies is the hunter clip. The hair is left on the legs, the saddle patch and you can leave the head unclipped if you wish or if the pony objects to having clippers around his face.

Leaving the legs hairy will give the pony some protection but you do need to check carefully for thorns or cuts especially after you've ridden across country.

With both full and hunter clips the horses need rugging up. You will need blankets too with extra ones at night. If you turn the horse out for an hour or so in the field he'll need a good New Zealand rug, possibly with an extra blanket underneath if the weather turns really cold.

LEFT, MAIN PICTURE: A hunter clip.

LEFT, INSET: Marking out a saddle patch with saddle soap or tailor's chalk.

Not all animals do enough work to warrant an extensive clip but still sweat up under the belly and around the chest. With these a blanket clip is ideal. Hair is removed from the neck, chest, belly and part way up the flanks leaving a blanket of the horse's winter coat over his back and loins.

Again these ponies need to be stabled, with rugs and equipped with a New Zealand if they spend some of the day outside. It would not be fair to give a pony a blanket clip and expect him to spend all day outside, even with the protection of a New Zealand rug.

A popular choice for animals doing light work (mainly hacking with the occasional competition), is the trace clip. Here the hair is removed from the belly along a horizontal line low down the sides — where the traces fitted on harness horses. Underneath and along the sides of the neck are also clipped.

With this type of clip you can turn a pony out all day, preferably with a New Zealand rug, but he ought to be stabled at night.

If your pony has to live out all year it is still possible to clip him a little. Just remove the hair from under his neck and around his chest so giving him a bib clip.

Ready to start

Before you clip give your pony a week or so of thorough grooming to clean his coat. You will not be able to do a very good job if the pony is wet, muddy or greasy.

If your pony has never been clipped before or is not too keen on the idea spend a couple of weeks running the clippers near him but not actually touching him. Let him investigate the switched off clippers and talk to him as you stroke his neck and body with them. If possible let him hear other ponies being clipped.

When you clip for real have someone standing near his head to comfort him. Just clip a small area at a time at first, especially if he's really nervous. You'll probably find he'll sweat up anyway in which case you'll have to wait until he's dry and cool again before continuing.

As with anything connected with horses, kindness combined with firmness and patience, will bring rewards. Twitching a pony to clip him might get the job done this time but next time you could find yourself with a real battle on your hands.

With very difficult animals you can ask your vet to tranquilise them but even this may not prevent a pony from misbehaving.

The majority of horses will accept being clipped quite readily providing they are introduced to it properly.

If possible clip in a stable, allowing yourself plenty of time and within daylight hours as this makes the job easier.

You may have to clip outside in which case it is even more important to have a rug close by to throw over the horse as his coat is removed.

Take any bedding out of the stable, replacing it with rubber matting if this is available. The floor should be dry, and your clippers properly earthed.

Clipping can be quite an itchy business so wear overalls over your clothers and keep your hair out of the way with a scarf.

Marking out the clip

Once the pony has been prepared for clipping — (groomed and his tail bandaged) — you can mark out the outline of the clip you have chosen using tailor's chalk or saddle soap.

With trace and blanket clips be careful to get both sides equal. For saddle patches put your own saddle on the horse and draw round it, leaving half an inch extra all round. For the legs you can follow the natural line of the forelegs and draw a slightly sloping diagonal line from the stifle to the back of the thighs when attending to the hindlegs.

For hunter and full clips draw a V upside down at the top of the tail.

The Clipping Process

To clip properly the blades of your clippers need to be at the correct tension. The manufacturer's instructions should be consulted — remember that if you have the blades too tight they will become hot and blunt much quicker. A spare pair of blades is not too expensive and should be kept handy.

Having tied up the pony quite short and tested the clippers it's time to start. Oil the clipper blades while they are moving so that the working parts are well lubricated.

Stroke the clippers along the horse's neck, then hold them away from him and start them. Hold your hand in between the clippers and the pony's neck so he can feel them vibrating.

Providing all is well you can then start to clip, beginning with an easy area such as the neck. Use long sweeping strokes against the lay of the coat. Do not push the clippers along, let the weight of the clipping head provide the pressure.

Leave the difficult bits until last and then ask someone to hold out the horse's foreleg so the skin behind the elbow is stretched tight. This makes it easier to clip without nicking the pony.

Ticklish bits such as under the belly can also be tackled with help. It may be necessary to have someone hold up a foreleg to stop the pony from kicking out while you clip along the belly. Stand close to the horse when you do this, resting your free hand on his back and talking soothingly to him.

Take care as you clip near the mane — you do not want to take chunks out of the mane roots. With the legs don't try to use clippers along the back of the tendons and the fetlocks. These can be trimmed later using a comb and scissors.

It's not worth arguing if your pony dislikes the clippers near his head. Hand operated ones can be used or just tidy up by using scissors — any scissors used on horses must be blunt ended for safety.

As you clip make a point of regularly checking that the blades are not too hot or becoming blunt. An old dandy brush is great for cleaning out the clippers — keep some light oil close by to squeeze onto the blades occasionally.

You can also use a body brush at regular intervals to remove any prickly loose hair from your horse. Sponge around the eyes, nostrils and dock to get rid of any stray hairs.

For the few days after clipping tiny bristly hairs will be growing through again so for your horse's added comfort use a cotton summer sheet under his rug.

6. FEEDING by Dr. Janice Harland, Equine Nutritionist

Feeding a horse is frequently described as both an art and a science. This is, of course, correct but for too long the emphasis has been on the art, while the science has been forgotten.

Nutrition as a science is well understood and the nutritional requirements of horses, although not absolutely perfect, are clearly defined.

To understand the science of nutrition and how to feed your horse according to his nutritional requirements let's begin by looking at the digestive system.

Digestion is quite simply the process by which feeds that contain proteins, fats and complex carbohydrates are broken down into units small enough to be absorbed and converted into a form useful to the horse.

Digestion occurs with the help of enzymes which are organic catalysts that speed up the biochemical processes involved in disgestion.

The digestive system

The main areas of the digestive tracts are the mouth, oesophagus, stomach, duodenum, ileum, caecum, colon, rectum and anus.

LEFT: Whatever activity your horse does he'll need the correct food — even if he's not working he'll need some maintenance rations.

Mouth

Digestion starts in the mouth but, at this stage, it is mainly mechanical — mastication and chewing of the food helps to break up the large particles of food. The teeth are very important in the breakdown of food and should be periodically examined and any sharp edges rasped down.

In the mouth the food is mixed with saliva (99 per cent water, one per cent mucin and mineral salts). This acts as a buffer, a lubricant and helps the food on its journey down the digestive tract.

Oesophagus

The gullet is the tube which links the mouth to the stomach. It is not very wide in diameter and may become blocked when a greedy horse bolts dry feed, or swallows a large piece of apple or carrot too quickly. This causes the horse to choke, which can be very serious if the obstruction is not removed.

You can avoid the danger by either moistening the feed or mixing in chaff to encourage the horse to chew and by chopping large carrots etc lengthways.

Stomach

True digestion begins in the stomach by the action of the gastric juices. These juices consist mainly of water, with mineral salts, mucus, hydrochloric acid and the enzyme precursor pepsinogen. The action of the acid on

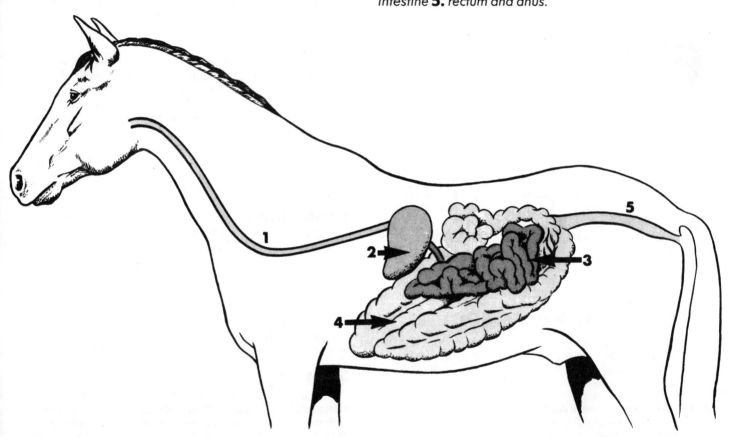

1. oesophagus **2.** stomach **3.** small intestine **4.** large intestine **5.** rectum and anus.

the enzyme precursor converts it to pepsin which starts the process of protein breakdown.

Protein is broken down into smaller chains of peptides and the individual blocks of proteins known as amino acids. Food does not stay long in the stomach. It may be on its way to the small intestine in as little as 20 minutes.

Small Intestine

This is where the real action is! Here the food is broken down into amino acids and simple sugars which are then absorbed into the blood stream.

Digestion of carbohydrates and fats starts here and protein digestion continues. The main enzymes involved in the digestive processes are found in either the pancreatic juices or intestinal juices. Bile produced by the liver contains no enzymes but converts the fat from large globules to tiny particles on which digestion can start.

After the many enzymes have done their stuff, the simple sugars and amino acids are absorbed across the wall of the small intestine, whilst the other food residues continue on their way to the caecum.

Large Intestine

The caecum is the first part of the large intestine and here many millions of bacteria and protozoa live. These tiny microbes contain enzymes which the horse itself does not possess. The enzymes can break down cellulose and hemi-cellulose which, along with lignin, are the main constituents of grass and hay.

The microbes are essential for fibre digestion, without them the horse could make little use of it. The microbes and enzymes can also digest any left over proteins, fats and carbohydrate and synthesize some of the B vitamins.

The colon is the site of absorption of water, electrolytes and the products of microbial digestion. Unfortunately it is not as efficient as the small intestine and the fibre is digested with an efficiency of only 25-35 per cent.

The colon is also badly designed in that it has a right angled bend in it which is very narrow. This is where colic usually occurs. The colic may be caused by large particles of food getting stuck or by the passage being partially blocked, so that the gas produced by microbes during their metabolism cannot escape quickly enough.

Colic can be caused by inadequate water supply, irregular feeds and extra large feeds. All of these can be avoided by good stable management.

Rectum and anus

The waste materials of digestion, namely water, undigested food residues, digestive juices, mineral salts, cells from the digestion tract itself and microbial cells and other products of bacterial decomposition, all go to form the faeces (droppings) which are stored in the rectum and pass through it to be finally voided via the anus.

The condition of the droppings and the frequency of their passage is often an indicator of the general well being of the horse. Any alteration in appearance may be a warning that something is wrong.

Nutrition

Now we know what digestion is about, let's turn to nutrition, which is basically balancing the nutrient supply to the horse's requirement. In other words, matching input to the required output.

In order to do this, we need to know what individual feeds contain and match their contents to the horse's requirements for each individual nutrient. A balanced diet must contain the following essential nutrients:

Carbohydrates

Fats

Proteins

Minerals

Vitamins

Water

Carbohydrates and fats are the main energy sources in the diet. These are the fuels which are required to make your horse grow and run. Proteins are required for building up, maintenance and repair of tissue and hence are the most important for the growth and development of the foal, yearling and pregnant and lactating mare.

Minerals are required for a wide range of biochemical processes in the body. They are divided into major minerals and trace minerals.

Vitamins are organic compounds required in small quantities for normal growth and maintenance of animal life. They are divided into fat-soluble and water-soluble types.

Water is necessary for the shape and form of every cell and is present in every body fluid. It is a carrier for substances in and out of the body, for example saliva and faeces, and is essential to many digestive processes and metabolism.

It plays a vital role in regulating temperature (we all know how profusely you can sweat on a hot day), and is also a lubricant in joints and eyes. It transports sound, keeps organs moist, dissolves chemicals — in fact the list is almost endless. It is vitally important.

Did you know that over 50 per cent of the horse's weight is water, and this may be as high as 70-80 per cent in foals and younger horses?

The amount of water required depends on six factors: the age of the horse or pony, the level of total feed intake, the nature of the feed, the ambient temperature and humidity, amount of work done, illness.

In general younger horses and foals have a relatively higher water requirement. The total feed intake is also a reflection of the size of the horse or pony. Several studies suggest as a general guide — two to four litres of water per one kilogram feed (two to four pints of water per one pound feed).

For example, a 1,000 lb (500kg) horse consuming 20lb (10kg) of feed requires 40-80 pints (5-10 gallons) of water.

Water consumption is higher on a hay based diet than on a grain-hay mixed ration. This is because hay is bulkier and requires more saliva to moisten it and it is less digestible than grain.

A rise in ambient temperature from 55 degrees to 77 degrees F (13-25 degrees C) will raise water requirement by 15-20 per cent. An increase in humidity also increases water requirement as the horse sweats more profusely and this moisture must be replaced.

Although the amount of riding, exercise or work done by a horse may double the water requirement, (sweating greatly increases the horse's water demand) after heavy exercise a hot horse should only be allowed a small amount of water. After the horse has cooled off or been fed, then water should be made freely available.

Illness, in particular diarrhoea, greatly increases water needs and is often a cause of dehydration. As a general guide a mature horse in light exercise requires 10 gallons of water daily.

Remember, the water should always be clean and fresh. Stagnant water may contain parasites and lead to disease. Rivers and streams should contain at least a four inch depth of water if the horse is to drink freely.

But what happens if your horse does not get enough water? Firstly, reduced feed intake which decreases growth and performance. More seriously, lack of water can lead to colic. A 10 per cent reduction in water will result in these disorders, a 20 per cent reduction leads to death.

LEFT: Keep your feed in vermin proof bins and ensure that the feed room is kept clean. All feed bowls should be swilled out immediately after being used.

Make sure you measure the feed out so you know exactly how much your horse is receiving.

Tips on Watering

- Always ensure the water is clean and fresh.
- During the summer water requirement increases and therefore buckets must be filled more frequently.
- During winter check that ice has not formed on the surface of the bucket or trough.
- When you are travelling take a small quantity of molasses with you to put in the water. This encourages your horse to drink water which may taste quite different from that used in his home area.
- Never let a horse drink heavily before exercise or when he is very hot after hard work.
- Remember, water is essential.

Energy

After water, energy is the most important nutrient in the diet.

The key functions for which energy is required include the action of the heart and maintenance of blood pressure; transmission of nerve impulses; muscle tone; growth and power; maintenance of body temperature; secretion of milk; protein and fat synthesis; transport across membranes.

Basically energy is the horse's fuel. Without it, he will not function. The usual sources of energy are carbohydrates and fats. Fats are currently not used to any great extent in horse nutrition. Their role is being investigated for high performance and endurance horses, where energy requirements are high as fats contain approximately two-and-a-quarter times more energy than a similar weight of carbohydrate.

All compounded nuts or cubes contain a certain proportion of fats, but this is generally only three to four per cent hence the role it plays is fairly insignificant. By far the most common source of energy is carbohydrates which include sugars (molasses), starch (cereals), cellulose and hemicellulose (hay and forages).

Energy is measured in megajoules which are the metric version of calories (4.184MJ is equivalent to 1 mega calorie). This may sound a little bewildering, but it's simple really. The diet-conscious will be quite used to counting the calories in food — in horse diets, it's simply a case of counting megajoules.

Not all the energy available in a food is used by the horse — that which is used is known as digestible energy (DE). You need to know the DE of each feedstuff so you can decide how valuable the feed will be to your horse.

You'll be able to find a breakdown of the contents on feed bags. Table one (see page 88) also gives you an idea for the DE values.

Ask a horse owner which is the best energising food and the answer will more than likely be oats. Yet other foods such as molassed sugar beet, barley and maize all have higher DE values.

The number of megajoules of DE of typical energy feeds used in horse diets are shown in Table 1.

Energy required

Having established how much energy a feed supplies, we now need to know the horse's energy requirement. This is more difficult to calculate as energy requirement depends upon weight, age, work done, environmental temperature and whether or not the animal is pregnant.

Weight

The horse's weight may be measured directly on a weighbridge or scale, or by measuring the girth. The girth measurement is closely related to liveweight and the table on page 89 shows the weight, in relation to girth measurement.

Age

If a horse is mature and doing no work, then the basic energy requirement to keep it alive is called the maintenance requirement.

Energy requirement at maintenance = 20MJ + 5MJ/50kg of horse liveweight.

For example a 400kg horse maintenance requirement is $20MJ + 5MJ \times \dfrac{400}{50} = 60MJ$ of digestible energy.

An immature horse requires additional energy for growth and development. Growth requires more energy than maintenance. Typical rates of growth for a foal are shown in Table 2.

Production

Both pregnancy and lactation require extra DE too. The energy requirements are:

Pregnancy (last 90 days) = maintenance + 12%
Lactation (up to 3 months) = maintenance + 30%
Lactation (from 3 months) = maintenance + 15%

For example a 400kg mare 10 days prior to foaling requires 60MJ for maintenance (see above)
$+ \dfrac{60}{100} \times 12 = 7.2$ Total: 67.2 MJ DE

What happens if there is not enough energy in the diet?

If there is insufficient energy available in the form of carbohydrate and fats, then protein is utilised as an energy source. This is inefficient and undesirable, as energy is actually used up in the breakdown of protein for energy. If the horse is in severe energy deficiency the metabolites produced may build up in the body and act as poisons.

A horse suffering from energy deficiency is lethargic and unwilling to participate in any activity. He will quickly lose condition and weight and his appearance will be dull and lifeless.

It is possible to accurately calculate the horses energy requirement in MJ of DE, feed a ration containing the correct number of MJ and yet the horse loses weight. Often this is because oats are being fed and they cause the horse to "heat up." Instead of the energy being transferred to the horse and used efficiently it is wasted by the horse being frisky and losing energy as nervous energy.

Oats are, therefore, said to contain "heating" energy, replacement of them by non-heating energy feeds means more efficient use of the diet by the horse, a quieter temperament and a happier rider who is not constantly fighting for control.

Good sources of non-heating energy are molassed sugar beet feed and Bailey's non-heating feeds. If you have a horse which is difficult to control and tends to hot up include one of these feeds in the diet.

What happens if there is too much energy in the diet?

Basically the horse gets fat, just as you or I do if we consume too many calories. So more is definitely not better!

Once you have established the correct feeding regime, your horse should maintain a fairly constant bodyweight. Regular bodyweight checks will indicate if you are over-feeding, or underfeeding, although weight loss may also be the indicator of a more serious disease or disorder.

Accurate ration formulation is a good start to getting your horse or pony in optimum condition, but it is not a substitute for good horsemanship.

The energy requirements are a good guide but may need fine tuning for your particular animal. If you have a pony which tends to run to fat, then you may need slightly below the calculated requirements whereas a thoroughbred may require slightly above the normal requirements. Learn to judge the horse's condition by good observation but support your instinct with accurate rationing.

Table 1

Dry matter and energy content (DE/kg Dry Matter) of energy feeds commonly used for horses.

	Dry Matter Per cent	DE MJ/ kg DM
Medium hay	86	10.2
Good hay	86	11.0
Poor hay	86	8.7
Oats	86	14.0
Barley	86	15.1
Maize	86	16.1
Molassed sugar beet feed	90	14.5
Molasses	75	14.0
Bailey non-heating horse feed	90	14.9

Table 2

Daily Gain in kg of growing horses

Age (months)	Horses mature weight	400kg (880lb)	500kg (1100lb)	600kg (1300lb)
3		1.0	1.1	1.25
6		0.65	0.80	0.85
12		0.40	0.55	0.60
18		0.25	0.35	0.35
42		0	0	0

Work done

The amount and type of work done can greatly increase the energy requirement. If we compare the horse to an athlete for a moment, everyone knows that a few days before the marathon a runner has to eat lots of carbohydrates, bread, jam, cakes, etc., to boost his energy reserves; similarly prior to heavy or prolonged exercise the horse's diet has to be gradually increased in energy content.

If your horse is only exercised at weekends then

start increasing the energy level of the diet on Friday, feed the higher energy ration on Saturday and Sunday and tone down the ration towards the normal level on Monday. By feeding in this manner the horse has energy reserves to do the additional work you are asking. The amount of energy required various according to the level of work:

For each hour of work add the following amounts of DE/50kg bodyweight

Light Work (roadwork and hacking) **1MJ DE.**
Medium Work (some cantering or light jumping) **3MJ DE.**
Hard Work (Cantering, galloping, jumping) **5MJ DE.**
Fast Work (racing) **7MJ DE.**

Horses in hard or fast work, such as hunting, eventing, jumping or pony club games, require a much greater amount of energy in the ration. Remember, energy is the fuel — the faster you go, the more you need.

Temperature

In cold and wet conditions the energy requirement is even higher to maintain body temperature. Therefore, if the horse is outwintered, remember to increase the energy content of the diet.

The maintenance requirements of a mature horse can generally be met by the forage in the ration — grass in the summer or good quality hay or Horsehage in the winter. For production or performance more energy-dense foods are required such as cereals, molassed sugar beet feed, and molasses, or in extreme cases fats such as maize, corn or soya bean oils.

Estimation of horse or pony bodyweight using girth measurement.

Pony

Girth in inches	40	42.5	45	47.5	50	52.5	55	57.5				
Girth in cm	101	108	114	120	127	133	140	146				
Bodyweight in lb	100	172	235	296	368	430	502	562				
Bodyweight in kg	45	77	104	132	164	192	234	252				

Horse

Girth in inches	55	57.5	60	62.5	65	67.5	70	72.5	75	77.5	80	82.5
Girth in cm	140	146	152	159	165	171	178	184	190	199	203	206
Bodyweight in lb	538	613	688	776	851	926	1014	1090	1165	1278	1328	1369
Bodyweight in kg	240	274	307	346	380	414	453	486	520	570	593	611

Table based on findings of Glushanok, Rochlitz and Skay 1981.

How do you put a ration together?

First we have to answer the following questions: weight (400kg), age (mature), production (none — not pregnant or lactating), work done (1 hour light work, 1 hour medium work), and environmental temperature (housed in stable).

The energy requirement is: maintenance plus 1MJ/50kg liveweight (light work) plus 3MJ/50kg liveweight (medium work)

$$\text{ie. } 60 + 1 \times \frac{400}{50} + 3 \times \frac{400}{50}$$
$$= 60 + 8 + 24$$
$$= 92\text{MJ DE}$$

How much will my horse eat?

The amount of feed dry matter (total weight of feed minus the water content) that a horse will eat is generally 1.5-2.5 per cent of its bodyweight, although it may be as high as 3 per cent in foals.

Typically horses consume 2 per cent of their bodyweight.

Horses dry matter intake = 2kg per 100kg bodyweight (21lbs per 100lb bodyweight).

For example a 400kg horse will consume 2 x 4kg of feed dry matter i.e. 8kg.

What feeds are available?

For our hypothetical 400kg horse we have the following feeds: oats (dry matter) 86 per cent, DE value (MJ) 14; molassed sugar beet feed (dry matter) 90 per cent, DE value (MJ) 14.5; hay (dry matter) 86 per cent, DE value (MJ) 10.2.

Therefore we need to pick a combination of these feeds which will meet the horse appetite of 8kg dry matter, but also provide 92MJ DE (Table 3):

Table 3

	Fresh Wt (kg)	x Dry % Matter	Dry Weight	x DE MJ in DM	= DE in Ration
Oats	2	86	1.7	14	23.8
Molassed Sugar Beet Feed (Weight Before Soaking)	1.25	90	1.1	14.5	16.0
Hay	6	86	5.2	10.2	53.0
Total			8.0		92.8

Therefore the combinations of feeds meet the horse's requirement for energy and dry matter intake. If these two factors are right, the rest of the ration usually falls into place. However, it is also necessary to take into account the protein requirements of the horse.

Proteins

Proteins are found in all living cells where they are intimately involved in all the activities which mean life to the cell. Eash tissue, organ or organism has its own particular protein; therefore, in nature, there are a large number of different proteins. For example, the protein in skin is different to the protein in liver, milk, beans, grass or indeed to any other protein.

The horse continually uses protein to build new tissues in the young growing foal and the pregnant and lactating mare or for repairing worn-out or damaged tissue in mature horses.

Protein is the main constituent of organs and tissues, such as muscle, blood, liver and kidneys. It is also needed to form hoof, hair, hormones, enzymes and most constituents of the body. Protein, therefore, affects most, if not all, bodily functions and also helps provide resistance to disease.

Proteins are made from amino acids. Earlier we explained how protein had to be broken down to amino acids in the small intestine before the horse could put the protein to use. It is, therefore, the individual amino acids which are important, rather than the whole protein. There are 25 amino acids in nature, 22 of which are required by the horse. These are divided into two types; non-essential amino acids can be synthesized by the horse itself. It can manufacture these amino acids as body functions demand. There are 10 essential amino acids which cannot be synthesized by the horse and must be provided in the diet if the horse is to remain healthy. A deficiency of just one of the essential amino acids can lead to a serious reduction in health and performance. Usually, lysine is the first limiting essential amino acid and it is particularly important to ensure that there are adequate quantities of it in the diet.

Proteins contain various quantities and combinations of non essential and essential amino acids. Better quality proteins contain a higher percentage of essential amino acids. The best protein available in nature is casein, found in milk. As milk is the sole feed of the new-born foal, it is essential that it contains the right balance of amino acid for growth and development.

The protein content of feeds is described as crude protein and expressed as a percentage of the feed.

Table 4 shows the crude protein content of feeds commonly used for horses. The lysine content is given as an indicator of the quality of the protein; as mentioned earlier, it is often this amino acid which limits performance and therefore the higher the lysine level, the better the protein.

Hay, oats and cereals generally are poor sources of lysine and a diet based solely on these feeds contains inadequate lysine for a growing horse. The diet should contain 0.6-0.7 per cent lysine for foals and 0.4-0.5 per cent lysine for yearlings. Mature horses need 0.4 per cent lysine in the diet.

It is advisable when selecting a vitamin mineral supplement to choose one which also contains lysine and preferably methionine and tryptophan, which are usually the next limiting amino acids. There should be a breakdown of content on the feed packet.

How much protein does my horse require?

We have already seen that the horse cannot obtain all the energy from a feed, as a proportion is lost in the faeces droppings. The quantity of energy the horse actually uses is called the Digestible Energy (DE). The protein situation is similar, a quantity of the protein is lost in the faeces and the usable portion is known as the digestible crude protein (DCP). The quantity of DCP in the feed is expressed as a percentage of the feed or in grams per kilogram. 10 per cent DCP is equivalent to 100 grams per kilogram.

When we talked about energy we first had to establish the maintenance requirement — the amount required by the horse to keep it ticking over. We have to do the same for protein.

Mature horses and ponies at maintenance require 8.5 per cent crude protein in diet.

Exercise, whether fairly gentle hacking or strenuous racing, requires very little extra protein — unlike energy, protein is not a fuel. Therefore, the requirement for it does not increase with additional effort.

Mature horses-
in light work
require 8.5-10 per cent crude protein in diet
in medium work
require 8.5-10 per cent crude protein in diet
in intense work
require 8.5-10 per cent crude protein in diet

Growing youngsters have a greater requirement for protein because they are building up body tissue:-

Foals (up to 6 months)
require 18 per cent crude protein in diet
Foals (6 to 12 months)
require 16 per cent crude protein in diet
Yearlings (first 6 months)
require 13-14 per cent crude protein in diet

Yearlings (next six months)
require 11-12 per cent crude protein in diet
Two year olds
require 10-11 per cent crude protein in diet

Pregnant and lactating mares require higher protein levels in the diet because they are building up tissue in the foetus and produce high protein milk for the foal:-

Pregnant Mares (last 3 months)
require 11 per cent crude protein in diet
Lactating Mares (first 3 months)
require 14 per cent crude protein in diet
Lactating Mares (next 3 months)
require 12 per cent crude protein in diet

If we compare the protein requirement for mature horses in work with the level of protein in most of the energy feeds listed in table 4, you will see the two compare quite closely.

For your average horse or pony hacking for an hour or two a day no supplementary protein is required, so forget the linseed, soyabean meal, and meat and bone meal — use it only for youngstock and brood mares.

As a balanced protein supplement, linseed does not compare favourably with soyabean meal. On average, linseed contains only 1.1 per cent lysine. If you are feeding linseed, perhaps you should examine your motives. Is it because it makes the horse's coat glossy? If this is the case, why not consider using molassed sugar beet feed, which has a similar effect but provides energy to the diet rather than protein which, in most cases, is not required. It is also much cheaper and easier to prepare — simply soak for 12-24 hours. The condition of the horse's coat is often a reflection of its state of health. A poor coat may be the result of an unbalanced diet or simply poor grooming. I'm afraid there really is no alternative to hard work on this one.

Checking the ration contains adequate protein.

We have already calculated that a 400kg horse, doing one hour's light work and one hour's medium work, needs the following amounts of feeds to meet its appetite and energy requirements. Let's see if it meets the requirement for protein.

Kg		%CP	KgxCP%	%Lysine	KGx% Lysine
6	Hay	8.5	51	0	0
2	Oats	10.9	21.8	0	0
1.25	Molassed Sugar Beet Feed	11.0	13.8	0.7	0.88
9.25	Total		86.6		

Total CP Intake = 86.6 average crude protein
Total intake   9.25 Content of diet
             = 9.4

Total CP Intake = 0.88 average lysine
Total intake   9.25 Content of diet
             = 0.1

At 9.4 per cent the protein content of the diet is well in excess of the required 8.5 per cent. The lysine content is rather low and it would be advisable to include a supplement containing lysine. Including a high protein feed like linseed would be undesirable as the total protein content of the ration would end up far too high.

What happens if the protein content of the diet is too low?

The appetite of the horse becomes depressed and the result is poor growth, loss of weight, reduced milk production if the mare is lactating loss of condition and reduced ability to work.

Because of the higher protein requirements of young growing horses and lactating mares, a protein deficiency quickly becomes apparent; however, with mature animals, the horse can apparently perform normally for a much longer period.

What happens if protein is overfed?

It is definitely not a case of more protein being better. Excess protein can lead to quite serious consequences in terms of performance.

It has been recognised for some time that excess protein can lead to excessive sweating (including breaking out syndrome). It may also result in higher pulse and respiration rates, indicating that the horse is under some stress. Crude protein levels of 15-17 per cent have been shown to induce these systems in mature animals with a normal requirement of only 8.5 — 10 per cent protein. A further factor observed was reduced feed efficiency and greater loss of water in the urine and faeces. The greater water loss can impose stress on the kidneys and lead to damage long term.

   The combination of high protein and low energy in the diet is particularly undesirable and leads to poor utilization of the ration. This is because the excess protein is metabolised and used as an energy source. The processes involved in this conversion require energy. So protein is metabolised to provide energy which in turn costs energy — extremely wasteful for both the horse and its use of the diet.

   Protein is not energy, there are very definite requirements for both. They are not interchangeable — make sure your ration has the right quantities of each.

   There are primarily two aspects of the harm caused by excess protein. Firstly, it is harmful to the horse and its performance. A recent study in America showed that every 1000g excess protein caused a racehorse to be 1-3 seconds slower. Can you imagine the reaction if a horse lost the race because too much protein was fed? If we look at the human parallel again, the athlete requires no supplementary protein to make him run races — this is a fact well researched.

   Secondly, harmful to your purse, because feeding excess protein is expensive in its own right, but, as it also leads to reduced feed efficiency by the horse, then the horse needs to eat more to get the same benefit. More food means more money. The fact that the horse is producing more urine and wetter droppings leads to a greater requirement for bedding which in turn is more expense in shavings, straw or paper and more effort in mucking-out for you

   Formulating a ration with the right amount of protein relies on having accurate information on the feeds available to you.

Table 4
Crude protein content of commonly used feeds.

	Crude Protein %	Digestible Crude Protein %	Lysine %
Energy Feeds			
Medium Hay	8.5	3.9	—
Good Hay	10.0	5.8	—
Poor Hay	4 - 8	2 - 3	—
Oats	10.9	8.4	—
Barley	10.8	8.2	0.4 approx
Maize	9.8	7.8	0.3 approx
Molassed Sugar Beet Feed	11.0	8.0	0.7
Molasses (Beet)	12.0	6.0	—
Protein Feeds			
Soyabean meal	50.0	45.3	3.3 approx
Feed beans	26.5	21.0	1.6 approx
Feed peas	26.2	22.5	1.5 approx
Skim milk powder	35.5	33.4	2.7
Linseed	26.0	20.8	0.8 approx
Linseed cake	33.2	28.6	1.1 approx
Meat & Bone meal	52.5	41.0	2.7
Others			
Bailey Horse Feed	15.0	11.5	0.3 approx
Wheat Bran	15.0	12.6	0.6 approx
Chaff	4 - 6	0.5-1.0	—

The protein content of hays can be very variable and it is advisable to get your hay analysed or only buy it from a feed merchant who has information relating to the crude protein content. Learn to read the labels on horse and pony cubes; every manufacturer by law has to give the protein content. It's the quality of the protein that's important and not the quantity so a 10 per cent CP horse and pony cube is not necessarily better than a 14 per cent CP product.

By changing from one hay to another or one brand of cubes to another, the protein balance of the ration can be severely upset. Similarly the variation in the protein content of good or bad oats is also large. So, buy from a reputable supplier who can provide all the information you require.

The high protein supplements such as soyabean meal, peas, beans, linseed, meat and bone meal and skim milk only have a place in the rations of breeding and young stock. So do not overload your horse or pony's system with these supplements. It's better for the horse and your purse without them!

Minerals

There are 16 minerals considered essential to the horse. Minerals are required for almost every biological process in the body, including the formation of the structure of the body, for example, bone. They are also involved as co-factors on many enzymatic reactions and act with vitamins, hormones and amino acids. Although these minerals are essential for life, an excess can cause severe health problems.

Minerals are present, in varying quantities, in nearly all feeds. The mineral content for hay will depend on the type of soil it was grown in, the amount of fertilizer it received, the species of grass, the stage of growth when harvested and the conditions of harvest.

Hay from particular areas of the country may be prone to a particular mineral deficiency due to the peculiarity of soil type. Other manufactured feeds, such as molassed sugar beet, have a constant mineral level because the processing it undergoes leads to consistency, whereas horse and pony cubes and coarse mixes are specially formulated to consistent mineral contents.

In addition, there are a number of mineral supplements available commercially. But beware, do not use more than the recommended levels, and not more than one supplement at once. For example. limestone flour is a good natural source of calcium — there is no need to feed it along with a synthetic calcium or general purpose mineral supplement, which inevitably contain calcium.

The mention of calcium brings us nicely to the first major element.

Calcium

This is the most abundant mineral in the horse's body and is an important constituent of the skeleton and teeth, in which 99 per cent of total calcium is found. It is also required for a number of enzyme reactions, the transmission of nerve impulses and the clotting of blood.

Bone consists of 46 per cent minerals and, of this, 36 per cent is calcium and 17 per cent phosphorus. Therefore, clearly, calcium levels in the diet are very important in foals and yearlings where the bones are still growing and also in pregnant and lactating mares, which are providing for their young.

A mature horse requires 45mg calcium/kg bodyweight, (equivalent allowance in the diet is 0.4 per cent), whereas a pregnant mare requires half as much again and a lactating mare two and a half times as much.

If calcium is deficient in the diet of young horses, then bone formation is impaired and the condition rickets is seen. The symptoms of rickets are mis-shaped bones, enlargement of the joints, lameness and stiffness. In adult animals, the bones become very weak and brittle and break easily.

In considering the calcium requirement of the diet, the calcium:phosphorus ratio also has to be considered. For optimum growth and development a ratio 1.5:1 calcium to phosphorus is required. Horses are tolerant to a 1:1 or 2:1 ration, but other ratios may lead to problems. The calcium to phosphorus ratio of commonly used feeds is given in Table 5 below.

Table 5
Calcium and Phosphorus Contents and Ratio of Commonly Used Feeds.

	Calcium	Phosphorus	Ca:P Ratio
	% in dry matter		
Hay	0.2-0.45	0.2-0.3	—
Oats	0.09	0.33	0.3:1
Barley	0.09	0.35	0.3:1
Maize	0.02	0.25	0.1:1
Molassed Sugar Beet Feed	0.9	0.09	10.0:1
Beet Molasses	0.07	0.07	1.0:1
Soyabean meal	0.25	0.58	0.4:1
Feed beans	0.14	0.57	0.2:1
Feed peas	0.07	0.40	0.2:1
Skim Milk Powder	0.10	1.00	1.1:1
Linseed Cake	0.38	0.75	0.5:1
Meat & Bone Meal	9-12	4-4.5	—
Baileys Horsefeed No. 1	0.24	0.28	0.9:1
Wheat bran	0.16	0.84	0.2:1
Limestone	38	0	—
Dicalcium phosphate	25	20	1.3:1

Most feeds contain too high a level of phosphorus, with the exception of molasses sugar beet feed, which can help to balance the mineral content.

Sources of calcium are ground limestone, dicalcium phosphate and bone meal. Feeds rich in calcium are meat and bone meal, green leafy crops, particularly legumes, and molassed sugar beet feed.

Phosphorus

The role of phosphorous in the diet is closely linked to that of calcium and 80 per cent of the total body phosphorus is found in the skeleton and teeth. Phosphorus also plays a significant role in carbohydrate metabolism and enzyme activation.

A mature horse requires 30mg phosphorus/kg

bodyweight and a daily allowance of 0.3 per cent in the diet is recommended. Like calcium, the requirement for phosphorus is highest in young and breeding horses and required levels increase in line with calcium in order to maintain the 1.5:1 ratio.

A deficiency of phosphorous is rare in stabled horses, but may occur if the horse is grazing poor quality weathered grass and given no supplementary feed. The symptoms are poor appetite and depraved appetite, for example, chewing foreign materials such as rags, bone, stones and wood. In young animals, deficiency can lead to rickets, stiff joints and muscular weakness. In breeding horses, fertility may be impaired.

Sources of phosphorus are dicalcium phosphate and bone meal. Feeds rich in phosphorous are cereals, bran and meat and bone meal.

Magnesium

Magnesium is closely associated to calcium and phosphorus, 70 per cent of it is found in the skeleton, the remainder is in the soft tissues and body fluids. Magnesium is the most common enzyme activator in the body. A mature horse requires 15mg mg/kg bodyweight, equivalent to a dietary allowance of 0.09 per cent.

Magnesium deficiency may occur on high grain low forage rations. The symptoms of deficiency are nervousness, muscle tremours and the horse is generally keyed-up and jumpy. Deficiency is unlikely to occur when the forage consists of more than 50 per cent of the diet. Excess magnesium upsets calcium and phosphorus metabolism.

Sources of magnesium are magnesium sulphate and oxide. Feeds rich in magnesium are wheat bran, linseed cake and vegetable protein concentrates.

Sodium & Chlorine (salt)

As chlorine is closely associated to sodium in the body, we will review their roles together. Most of the sodium is present in the soft tissues and body fluids. The regulation of body fluids is the main role of these elements. Sodium is also important in muscle contraction and the manufacture of bile. Chlorine forms part of the hydrochloric acid found in the stomach. A horse requires 0.5-1.0 per cent salt in the diet.

A deficiency of salt is most likely to occur when the horse is sweating profusely as salt is an ingredient of sweat. This may be a result of hard exercise or environmental conditions.

Therefore, if a horse is exercised hard in warm conditions, it should be given additional salt. Deficiency of salt leads to muscle fatigue and heat stress. Over a longer period of time it can cause the coat to become rough and the hair to drop out, as well as reduce growth and poor appearance. Salt may be given as a rock salt lick or supplement to the diet.

Potassium

Along with sodium and chlorine, potassium plays an important role in the regulation of body fluids. It also plays a significant part in nerve and muscle activity and carbohydrate metabolism. The ration of a mature horse should contain 0.4 per cent potassium.

As the potassium levels of forage are very high, it is exceedingly unlikely that deficiency will occur when rations of 35 per cent or more forage are fed. An excess of potassium may make the animal become very loose and lead to diarrhoea.

Sulphur

Most of the sulphur in the horse's body occurs in proteins containing the amino acids methionine and cysteine.

You will remember earlier we established methionine was often the second limiting amino acid to performance.

Deficiency of sulphur is not normally considered as it would reflect itself specifically in the form of a protein deficiency. Therefore, if protein levels are adequate, and we have shown that most of the time they are more than adequate, then sulphur levels will also be acceptable.

The foregoing minerals are termed major elements as they are required in larger amounts than the group of minerals we will discuss next. These are needed in only very small quantities and are called trace minerals. The levels of trace minerals required are expressed in parts per million (ppm). Before moving to the trace minerals, let's check the calcium and phosphorous level of the diet we formulated in the 'Energy' section and look at the protein content. (See Table opposite).

As the table shows, our ration contains adequate calcium and phosphorus and the ratio is also within the accepted range. Therefore, no supplementary calcium and phosphorus is required. However, without the molassed sugar beet feed inclusion, the diet would have been severely calcium deficient.

400kg Horse (mature) doing one hour light work and one hour medium work, housed in stable.

Ration	Fresh Wt (kg)	Dry Wt (kg)	Ca g/kg	P g/kg	Ca in Feed	P in Feed
Oats	2	1.7	1	3	1.7	5.1
Molassed Sugar Beet Feed	1.25	1.1	9	1	9.9	1.1
Hay	6	5.2	3.5	2	18.2	10.4
					29.8	16.6
Ca:P ratio				1.8:1		

Requirement for calcium = 45 mg/kg bodyweight = 45 x 400 = 18000mg or 18g.

Requirement for phosphorus = 30mg/kg bodyweight = 30 x 400 = 12000mg or 12g.

Required Ca:P ratio 1:1 — 2:1 — actual 1.8:1.

Trace Minerals

Iron

More than 90 per cent of the iron in the body is combined with proteins, the most important of which is haemoglobin found in red blood cells. It is also a component of many enzymes and is stored in the spleen, liver, kidney and bone marrow. For mature horses, 40ppm iron is required in the diet. For foals the level required is higher, at 50ppm, and for horses subjected to very heavy exercise, for example racing, 80-100 ppm.

Iron deficiency leads to anaemia. It is therefore particularly important for foals to receive adequate iron as milk is a very poor source. The need for iron also increases when due to injury, there has been a lot of blood lost by the horse. A severe worm burden can increase iron requirements due to the bleeding caused internally. In most horses iron deficiency is exceedingly rare, but an excess of iron can lead to digestive disturbances.

Good sources of iron are ferrous sulphate, cane molasses and green leafy forages.

Copper

Copper, along with iron and vitamin B12, is required for haemoglobin formation. In young growing animals, it is also closely associated to normal bone formation. It plays a role in many enzyme systems and is necessary to promote normal hair pigmentation.

For mature horses, 5-8ppm copper should be present in the diet. For young foals, 8-10ppm copper is required.

Mares milk is low in copper and therefore deficiency symptoms are most frequently seen in foals, Deficiency results in anaemia and poor bone formation of young horses. Horses grazing severely copper-deficient pastures may also develop anaemia. Under normal circumstances, copper is widely distributed in foods. Seeds and seed by-products are usually rich in copper; molassed sugar beet is a good source — it contains 12ppm.

Copper may be toxic if fed at high levels over a period of time as it is a cumulative poison and builds up in the body tissues, particularly the liver.

Cobalt

Cobalt is required for the synthesis of vitamin B12 in the intestinal tract of the horse. All horses require 0.1ppm cobalt in the diet. This requirement is very low and deficiency disease is confined to areas where horses may graze low-cobalt pasture. Cobalt may be found at low levels in most feeds and proprietary mineral mixes also contain it.

Iodine

Iodine is required by the thyroid gland to produce a hormone called thyroxine which is responsible for controlling the rate of body metabolism and heat production. Iodine is required at 0.1ppm in the diet of horses.

A deficiency of iodine leads to enlargement of the thyroid gland which is in the neck. Reproductive failure is an indication of iodine deficiency in breeding animals. An excess of iodine may lead to enlargement of the thyroid and hence is toxic. Iodine occurs in traces in most foods but the richest sources are those of marine origin, namely, seaweed, fishmeal and plants and forage growing near the coast.

Salt is often iodised and mineral/vitamin supplements provide iodine to the diet.

Manganese

The amount of manganese in the horse's body is

extremely small, although it is found in most tissues where it is important as an enzyme activator. The role it plays is fairly similar to that of magnesium. All horses require 40ppm manganese in the diet.

A deficiency of manganese results in abnormal bone formation, lameness, shortening and bowing of legs and enlarged joints, poor growth results and, in breeding horses, impaired reproduction.

Most feeds contain manganese and therefore horses kept under normal conditions are unlikely to suffer deficiency. However, excessively high levels of calcium and phosphorus in the diet can decrease the absorption of manganese and upset the dietary balance.

Selenium

Selenium is associated with vitamin E in the body, where it helps to avoid muscle disorders, including muscular dystrophy. The selenium requirement of horses is 0.1ppm in the diet.

The horse is intolerant to high levels of selenium, which leads to poisoning. This manifests itself as loss of hair from the mane and tail. In severe cases, the hooves slough-off, lameness occurs, food consumption decreases and death may occur by starvation.

Zinc

Zinc is required in the diet for normal protein synthesis and metabolism. Zinc also imparts a gloss or bloom to the coat.

Horses require 40ppm zinc in the diet. Foals fed lower levels of zinc showed impaired rate of growth, poor feed efficiency, reduced appetite and rough, dull coat. But at levels of over 1000ppm in the diet, zinc is toxic to horses. Zinc is fairly widely distributed in most feeds, in particular in the bran and germ of cereals.

Molybdenum

Information relating to this element is sparce. It is required as a cofactor for one enzyme reaction and hence is classified essential. No deficiency symptoms have ever been recorded, but it may be toxic if present at high levels as it interferes with copper retention. No specific recommendation for molybdenum level in the diet is available.

Clearly, it is impractical to suggest you tot up the level of each individual mineral provided by each feed ingredient. To ease the burden of rationing and give you peace of mind, mineral/vitamin supplements were devised.

A large number are available commercially, each with slightly different mineral contents. Read instructions carefully and accurately weigh the mineral required. Do not use more than advised, otherwise you run the risk of problems with one of the many described toxicity diseases.

Check the mineral levels in the supplements against the guidelines given in this chaper. The figures are based on the National Research Council's values and hence any products should be providing similar levels to those recommended.

Horse and pony cubes and coarse mixes already contain minerals and vitamins. Therefore, if you are following the manufacturer's recommendations, no supplementary minerals/vitaimins are necessary.

If you feed horse and pony cubes along with other

straights such as oats, barley, bran, chaff, molassed sugar beet and molasses, then you are interfering with the mineral balance in the cubes and, because of the uncertain mineral content of most straight feeds, it is advisable to use a supplementary mineral/vitamin in this case.

Vitamins

Vitamins are complex organic compounds required in minute amounts by horses for normal growth and development.

They come in two groups — fat soluble and water soluble.

The fat soluble vitamins are A, D, E, and K, and the water soluble are Cobalmin (B_{12}), Biotin, Absorbic Acid (C), Choline, Folic Acid, Miacin, Pantothenic Acid, Riboflavin (B_2), Thiamine (B_1), Pyridoxine (B_6), Para-aminobenzoic acid and Inositol. The last two water soluble vitamins mentioned play a minor role in equine nutrition and they will not be discussed further. The units which are used to measure vitamin requirements are international units (IU/kg) and mg/kg.

The vitamin content of feeds varies according to the soil type, climatic conditions, harvesting and storage. High quality leafy green forage and sunshine give horses many of the vitamins they need, but deficiencies are most likely to occur when low quality forage is fed or high quantities of unsupplemented refined feeds are given. Additional vitamins may be necessary during drought conditions and when production is being forced or the horse is under stress.

As the quantities of each vitamin required vary, for simplicity the requirements are listed in Table 6 (page 106) for a typical horse diet.

We will start by discussing the role of the fat soluble vitamins in nutrition.

Vitamin A

In the early part of this century, the yellow pigment carotene (found in carrots) was shown to be essential for life and health. Latterly it was discovered that carotene and carotenoids are converted to vitamin A in the intestinal wall. Vitamin A was shown to be necessary for several body functions, including vision, the preservation of mucous membranes, growth and reproduction. It also helps in disease resistance.

If a deficiency occurs the first symptons are often reduced sight and eye damage leading to night blindness. Uneven and poor hoof development, poor growth, reproductive failure and lack of resistance to disease are other signs. Deficiency is most likely to occur during drought or when poor quality or old hay is fed, and the younger the horse, the more quickly vitamin deficiency will show up.

Good sources of vitamin A are green leafy forages and carrots. Table 7 (page 107) gives the carotine content of some commonly used feeds. It is wasteful, expensive and may be dangerous to feed excessive quantities of vitamin A, which leads to bone fragility and skin damage.

Vitamin D

The most effective D vitamin in equine nutrition is vitamin D_3 (cholecalciferol). It's main function is the absorption, transport and deposition of calcium and, to a lesser extent, phosphorus. A deficiency of vitamin D can produce rickets in a foal, even though the calcium and phosphorus levels are correct. Deficiency of vitamin D in mature animals leads to weak bones and large joints, stiffness of gait and general irritability.

Young growing horses need proportionately more vitamin D_3 than mature animals, but because of the risk of excess vitamin D_3 the allowances have to be assessed very carefully.

Excess vitamin D_3 in the diet leads to bone abnormalities, calcification of the blood vessels, heart and other soft tissues. Toxic levels of vitamin D_3 have not been established for the horse but in other species ten times the requirement is toxic.

The precursors of vitamin D are found in most forages. Exposure of the horse to sunlight converts these to active vitamin D_3. Deficiency of this vitamin is therefore most likely to occur when the horse is stabled all day

Vitamin E

Tocopheral is the compound with the highest vitamin E activity. The vitamin E is required primarily as an anti-oxidant. In this role, it prevents the oxidation of unsaturated lipid (fat) in the cells. If this oxidation were permitted to occur, it would lead to cell damage. Vitamin E also ensures the stability and maintenance of blood vessels and promotes the production of some hormones.

Deficiency of vitamin E may lead to muscle disease, making the horse weak and unable to walk or rise. It may also lead to poor reproductive performance and anhidrosis, a condition of poor, dull coat, elevated temperature and high blood pressure.

Vitamin E is found in most green forage and hay.

Generally speaking, rations should be adequate in vitamin E. But, if fat supplementation is taking place, vitamin E requirements rise, as shown in the footnote to Table 6.

Selenium may partially spare vitamin E, but can only fulfil part of the role which the vitamin plays. These two nutrients are very closely linked and adequate quantities of both are required for good health.

Vitamin K

Vitamin K is required for effective clotting of blood. A deficiency of this vitamin therefore leads to an increased time taken for blood to clot and, more seriously, the blood will not coagulate at all, leading to death by haemorrhaging.

Vitamin K is present in green forages, well cured hay and fish meal. As it is widely distributed in feeds, deficiency is comparatively rare and usually occurs after digestive disorders. There is evidence to suggest the microflora in the caecum and colon can also synthesise enough vitamin K to meet the horse's requirements.

Water soluble vitamins

Thiamine (B_1)

Thiamine was the first vitamin to be studied in detail. It was found that the disease beri-beri, seen in people eating polished rice could be prevented if the rice bran was added back to the diet.

Thiamine is an essential part of many enzyme systems, in particular those which regulate the release of energy from stored carbohydrate and fat.

Any shortfall in thiamine levels can be seen in terms of lack of energy, muscle weakness and cramp. A slight deficiency may lead to decreased feed consumption and thereby loss of weight, unco-ordination (especially in the hindquarters), weakness and diarrhoea.

Thiamine is found in green pastures, good quality hay and cereal grains and bran. Deficiency is most likely to occur when the horse is given poor quality hay and grain and where antibiotics are given, as they can affect the synthesis of several of the B vitamins.

Since carbohydrate metabolism is increased during exertion, it is important when the horse is in hard work that there is adequate thiamine in the diet.

Riboflavin (B$_2$)

Riboflavin was initially also extracted from rice bran and is essential for several functions within various enzyme systems. It is important in the metabolism of carbohydrates, proteins and fats. A deficiency of riboflavin leads to periodic ophthalmia (moon blindness), which leads to conjunctivitis in one or both eyes, accompanied by weeping or streaming of the eyes. It may also lead to weak and porous bones, decreased rate of growth and impaired feed efficiency.

Good sources of riboflavin are green forage, milk and milk products. Deficiency will generally occur only when green forages are not available.

Niacin (B$_3$)

Niacin is the active group of two important co-enzymes which catalyse the transfer of hydrogen in the metabolism of proteins, fats and carbohydrates.

A deficiency of niacin is characterised by disorders of the skin, digestive organs and nervous system. The first signs of deficiency are loss of appetite, reduced growth, diarrhoea and other digestive disorders. As the deficiency becomes more serious, the skin may become scaly, the mouth ulcerated and nervous disorders become prevalent.

Extremely high levels of niacin in the diet can also cause a problem leading to increased heart beat and respiration rate.

Niacin is widely found in feeds, in particular, lucerne, animal by-products and oil seeds. There is evidence to suggest a small amount of synthesis of niacin in the digestive tract. If a balanced diet is being fed, niacin deficiency is unlikely to occur.

Pantothenic acid (B$_5$)

Pantothenic acid was first isolated from yeast and shown to be an essential part of co-enzyme A, which is at the centre of energy metabolism. It is also involved in the synthesis and degradation of fatty acids and in the formation of anti-bodies which help combat disease.

Loss of appetite and reduced growth rate are the first symptoms of deficiency, followed by dermatitis and skin disorders.

The synthesis of pantothenic acid in the gut should normally meet the horse's requirement for this vitamin. Grain is very deficient in pantothenic acid and when high grain diets are being fed, supplementation may be necessary.

Folic Acid

Folic acid is involved in the transfer of single

carbon units into larger molecules. This may be during the synthesis or degradation of specific amino acids or during nucleic acid formation. Anaemia and poor growth rate are the usual signs of deficiency.

Folic acid is widely found in horse feeds, in particular in green leafy plants. It is also synthesized in the gut of the horse so supplementation of the diet is not generally necessary, but may be considered good insurance.

Choline

Choline is essential in building and maintaining cell structure. It also plays a vital role in fat metabolism in the liver and in the transmission of nerve impulses. Retarded growth is the first symptom of deficiency, followed by increased deposition of fat, particularly in the liver.

Rations low in the amino acid methionine make the horse more likely to choline deficiency. Generally, as choline is found in a variety of feeding stuffs, in particular fish meals and vegetable proteins, deficiency is not widely seen, but may lead to reduced performance.

Pyridoxine (B$_6$)

Pyridoxine is involved in various enzyme systems which are acting in a large number of metabolic processes in the body. As a result of its action in these processes, pyridoxine is essential for energy production, fat metabolism, central nervous system activity and blood haemoglobin production. It also assists in disease prevention.

Because of the wide range of activities the vitamin takes part in, the symptoms of deficiency are non-specific. In acute deficiency, skin lesions and ulcers appear, nervous disorders and irritability become prevalent and anaemia may develop.

Pyridoxine works closely with other vitamins, namely, thiamine, riboflavin, niacin, absorbic acid, biotin and vitamin E. A deficiency of it may also affect pantothenic acid and vitamin B$_{12}$ mode of action.

Pyridoxine is widely found in feeds, bran is a particularly good source, and therfore deficiency is unlikely to occur when a balanced diet is being fed.

Vitamin B$_{12}$

For many years vitamin B$_{12}$ was known as the 'animal protein factor' as it is an essential part in many enzyme systems involved in the metabolism of protein. It also is essential for carbohydrate and fat metabolism. It's action is closely linked to folic acid.

Deficiency leads to loss of appetite and poor rates of growth. Nervous disorders and inability to co-ordinate may be seen if the deficiency persists.

Diets low in feeds of animal origin predispose the horse to deficiency — good sources of the vitamin are fish meals and meat and bone meals. The addition of B$_{12}$ to the diet of horses showing anaemia due to poor nutritional condition can improve the condition considerably.

Biotin

Biotin is one of the more recently discovered vitamins and until not long ago it was assumed that the horse could synthesize adequate quantities of biotin in the digestive tract. Recent research has shown that biotin deficiency can lead to soft hooves.

The complete role of biotin is not yet understood but it is essential for life, growth, food utilization, maintenance of epidermal tissues, normal bone development and reproduction. Thus indirectly, biotin is involved in the metabolism of carbohydrates, fat and proteins, in particular, the 'hard' protein keratin.

Deficiency of biotin leads to dry, scaly skin or a softening of the normally hard tissues, such as the hoof. The full aspects of biotin metabolism are as yet unknown. However, in a recent trial, five horses with a known history of foot disorders were given a biotin supplement and inspected regularly. At the beginning of the trial the hooves were weak and tended to crumble at their lower edges. The walls of the hooves were weak and thin with horizontal ridges. In addition, the soles were thin with low heels, shrunken and split frogs meant that the horses could not retain proper shoes and were unwilling or unable to walk over rough ground.

Most of the horses were given 15mg biotin/day for six months. After a few months of treatment the hooves had developed a better shape, the walls were tougher and thicker and the edges no longer crumbled. The horse moved better all round.

After six months of treatment, the dosage was halved and then discontinued. Hoof strength has been retained. As no specific requirement for biotin has been established, it is not possible to say whether or not the horses had been on a biotin deficient diet, but it seems that biotin may have a role to play in strengthening horse hooves for animals with a history of foot weakness.

Vitamin C (absorbic acid)

Sailors who had scurvy discovered that fresh fruits such as lemon or lime prevented the disease and, in essence, discovered the role which we now know vitamin C plays. Vitamin C is transported to all living cells where it takes place in oxidation and reduction reactions of cell metabolism. It also stimulates defensive mechanisms and plays an active role in the transport of iron.

It is assumed that the horse can synthesize adequate quantities of vitamin C, although it is not clear if this is the case. Supplementation of this vitamin is not normaly considered necessary.

Vitamin supplements — are they really necessary?

There is a wide range of vitamin/mineral supplements available on the market, none of which seem to be the same in either the quantity or number of vitamins which they supply. In general, a vitamin supplement is a good safeguard, but a single supplement fed at the recommended level is all that is required. In many situations, strictly speaking, a vitamin supplement is not necessary.

Choose the supplement you feed with your specific horse or pony in mind. For a horse or pony ridden an hour a day and doing light work, a broad spectrum supplement containing viramins A, D, and E is all that is necessary.

It is advisable to use a supplement containing the amino acid lysine, as discussed in the protein section. A supplement of this type would be a suitable addition to the ration we formulated earlier.

For pregnant and lactating mares and young stock, supplementation is more critical. Again, use a proprietary supplement formulated for the breeding horse or foal.

There are a number of supplements formulated for high performance horses. These are designed for racehorses, three day eventers and horses participating in endurance events, not for horses and ponies occasionally taking part in shows or gymkhanas. Therefore, stick to the cheaper, broad spectrum supplements. They are more than adequate for the child's or teenager's horse or pony.

When buying supplements, read the label carefully and follow the instructions given. Specific situations make supplementation more critical and these are outlined below.

1. Increased stress and sub-clinical levels (ie. not yet showing symptoms) of disease resulting from closer contact and confinement of horses.

2. The depletion of certain nutrients in soils leading to lower nutrient levels in forages.

3. Methods of handling and processing feeds can destroy vitamins.

4. Moulds in feeds increase certain vitamin requirements.

5. The presence of drugs, anthelmintics (ie. drugs acting against parasites) increase certain vitamin requirements.

6. Increased demands on the horse in terms of performance can increase vitamin requirements.

7. Certain nutrient inter-relationships can increase vitamin requirements.

8. Housing, and confining horses indoors, can also increase vitamin requirements

Table 6
Vitamin Supplementation required by horses.

	Total requirement	Supplement should provide
Vitamin A (IU/kg)	12,000	12,000
Vitamin D$_3$ (IU/kg)	1,200	1,200
Vitamin *E (mg/kg)	Up to 200	100
Vitamin K (mg/kg)	not known	1 (maximum)
Thiamine (mg/kg)	15	2**
Riboflavin (mg/kg)	15	3**
Naicin (mg/kg)	25	20**
Pantothenic Acid (mg/kg)	15	10
Folic acid (mg/kg)	10	1**
Choline (mg/kg)	200	100**
Pyridoxine (mg/kg)	10	2**
Vitamin B$_{12}$ (Ug/kg)	250	20**
Biotin (Ug/kg)	200	100
Vitamin C (mg/kg)	250	100**

* Vitamin E recommendations assume a maximum of 3 per cent fat in the diet. A further 5mg/kg Vitamin E should be added for each per cent fat above 3 per cent.

** In most cases the diet should contain adequate

quantities of these vitamins and specialist supplement products should not be required, unless the horse has been kept and fed in the conditions which are likely to predispose the horse to deficiency, as detailed in the text.

Table 7

	Vitamin A Carotene mg/kg	Vitamin E Tocopherol mg/kg
Ryegrass	260	40-100
Lucerne	180	37-110
Leafy grass hay	40	16-40
Mature hay	10-20	1-20
Carrots	890	1-5
Maize	2.5	4-18
Barley	0	2-14

Nutrition and Nutrition Related Diseases

Before discussing some commonly occurring diseases which have nutritional causes lets look at the role of fibre in the diet. Fibre is part of the carbohydrate fraction of the food and provides energy like other carbohydrates, namely, oats, barley, maize, molasses, etc. It also provides bulk and long fibre to ensure the well being of the digestive tract.

Recently a lot of publicity has been given to the F-plan diet for people, demonstrating the importance of fibre in human diets. Fibre is even more important for horses to keep their poorly designed digestive system in good working order. Insufficient fibre will lead to compacted feed in the digestive tract and eventually to constipation or colic. Conversely, if too much fibre is fed to high performance horses, they will have too much bulk in the ration and not enough energy so their performance will be limited.

Where does fibre in the diet come from?

The main sources of fibre are forages, bran, chaff and sugar beet feeds, although other feeds such as oats also contain a small percentage. Fibre is made up primarily from cellulose, hemicellulose, pentosans, (long chains of five carbon units) and lignin. The horse does not contain the enzymes necessary to break down fibre, but the bacteria in the caecum and colon do. Therefore, all the fibre is digested in the hind gut. It is broken down to volatile fatty acids, which can be converted to energy. Fibre is not digested very efficiently by the horse, consequently it does not provide a large amount of energy for high performance animals. The efficiency with which the fibre is digested depends on its digestibility or the 'D' value of the feed. The higher the 'D' value, the more the product is digested. A horse is unable to digest lignin and therefore forages rich in it are largely undigestible, for example, straw.

Table 8 (page 112) shows the fibre content (percentage crude fibre) and its digestibility coefficient of some feeds commonly given to horses. It can be seen that many feeds are only 35-50 per cent digestible which is the maximum the feeds can be used by the horse — the real value to the horse is probably less.

Molassed sugar beet feed is exceptional in containing fibre which is highly digestible, ensuring good use by the horse. Consequently, for high performance animals with high energy demands, feeding molassed sugar beet is a good way of ensuring adequate energy and fibre in the diet.

What levels of fibre are required in the diet?

The minimum recommendation for most types of horses is .5kg Fibre/100kg liveweight of horse (.5lbs Fibre/100lbs liveweight of horse).

This equates to 25 per cent of dry matter intake. Foals and growing horses may require slightly lower levels of fibre.

Clearly, the ratio of forage to concentrate varies in the diet, depending on the age, work-load and quality of the fibre or forage being fed. Poor quality roughage (low digestibility fibre) requires more supplementation than good forage (high digestible fibre).

A general guide to the optimum forage to concentrate ratios are given below.:

	Forage percentage	Concentrates percentage
No work*	100	0
Light work	75	25
Medium work	50	50
Hard work	30	70
Fast work**	25	75
Foal & brood mare	25	75

* Forage must be average to good in quality. A mineral/vitamin supplement is recommended in this instance.
** Poor quality forage is not suitable for fast work.

Checking the ration contains adequate fibre.

In the earlier part of this chapter, we formulated a ration for a 400kg horse doing one hour's light work and one hour's medium work a day. The ration was calculated to be 6 kg hay (average quality), 2 kg oats, 1.25kg molassed sugar beet feed, totalling 9.25kg.

The percentage forage in the diet is calculated from (forage(kg) ÷total(kg)) x 100 = (6÷9.25) x 100 = 65 per cent forage. 100 per cent − 65 per cent = 35 per cent concentrate.

This ratio is between the suggested forage to concentrate ratio for horses doing light and medium work. As our horse is doing both light and medium work, it is to be expected that the value would be mid-way between the ratios.

Forage digestion requires specific types of bacteria, whereas digestion of oats or cereals requires other bacteria to break them down. It takes approximately 7 to 14 days to build up the right number and type of bacteria to digest a diet efficiently.

Therefore, when you alter the diet it is important that the change is gradual to ensure you have the right quantity and type of bacteria in the gut. It also means if you are feeding say hay, horse and pony cubes and molassed sugar beet feed, then you should feed equal quantities of each ingredient at each meal throughout the day.

A mix of feeds is digested more efficiently than a single ingredient given at different times throughout the

day. This is because the bacteria are working unevenly. The horse is naturally a grazing animal and in nature eats small meals throughout the day, rather than big meals twice a day. Consequently, domesticated horses should be kept in a way which imitates as closely as possible the natural environment.

We have now covered the main scientific aspects of feeding however, these in isolation would not lead to a healthy horse. It is also important to practice good equine management—see the ten tips for better feeding management (page 112). You also need to worm horses regularly. The frequency of worming will depend of the size of the pasture and the number of horses on it. There are a number of proprietary worming powders available. In general terms a horse requires treatment every 8 to 12 weeks. On heavily infected pastures this may reduce to every 6 weeks during the spring/summer.

Sometimes you seem to have done everything right and still your horse develops one of the following disorders. Let us now try to investigate the reasons why these complaints occur and how to avoid them.

Colic

Colic is a very inspecific term, but, when used correctly, relates to severe or violent abdominal pain arising from the stomach or intestines.

Colic occurs frequently in horses because of the small size of the stomach, the horse's inability to vomit and the great size of the caecum and colon, with it's

LEFT: All ponies need good quality food in a balanced diet if they are to give of their best.

puckered surface which allows particles of food to become lodged.

The cause of colic is generally mismanagement. Namely, insufficient water, neglect of regularity of feeding, rapid changes in diet, feeding too large meals and inadequate worming. No specific feeds cause colic, but badly preserved forage, under-dried cereals, mouldy feeds or badly prepared mashes may all contribute. All feeds should be free of foreign objects as ingestion of these may lead to obstruction and cause colic.

Therefore, improved management is the key factor which can reduce the incidence of this disorder.

Diarrhoea

This may be caused as a result of excessive levels of protein in the diet, or a sudden change from one type of diet to another. It may also be an indication of a high worm burden in a the horse. A large intake of soil or sand with the diet can lead to diarrhoea.

If, after reducing or standardising the diet, diarrhoea persists, then get in contact with your local vet, particularly if the horse's temperature is raised as it may be a symptom of a more serious disease.

Azoturia (tying-up)

The horse never has an attack of this disease when at rest, but symptoms appear very soon after exercise has commenced, usually within a few hundred yards of starting. Diets high in starch, fed when the animal is at rest seem to predispose the horse to this condition and although the actual cause and effect is not fully understood, the condition appears to be caused by a build up of lactic acid.

Avoid this disorder by not over feeding concentrates when the horse is at rest. If the horse is to be exercised for the first time after a few days lay-off, break him in gently. Allow him to walk or graze initially, then gradually move into a trot and so on. In particular, don't expect your horse to perform immediately after you have transported him to a show or gymkhana, allow a little time to settle down and recover from the journey and his lay-off.

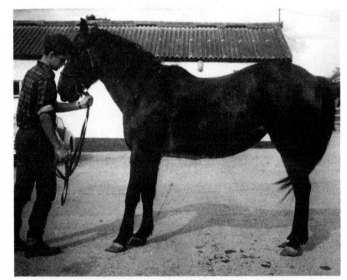

The typical stance of a pony suffering from laminitis — the animal is unwilling to put any weight on the forefeet.

Laminitis

Laminitis is a very painful condition affecting the feet. Native ponies and cobs are most prone to the disease although any horse can get it.

The actual cause and effect is not fully understood, although, once again, diets rich in starch seem to be the main cause. Often the disorder occurs in the spring, when the pony is turned out on to a very lush pasture full of soluble carbohydrate. The carbohydrate leads to excessive production of lactic acid which interferes with circulation in the foot.

To avoid this disorder, restrict grazing of ponies prone to this disease and do not feed supplementary concentrates which are rich in readily fermentable starch. For example, oats, barley, maize or horse and pony cubes. Use products like Bailey's non-heating meal and molassed sugar beet feed in small quantities.

If a pony is suffering from laminitis low level balanced diet is essential. Therefore, don't forget to feed mineral/vitamin supplements and the other nutrients required or else you will see symptoms of another type.

Overweight horses and ponies are more prone to this disorder, so keep your animal fit and trim and this will also help.

Choking

Is usually caused by the horse swallowing quickly a piece of carrot, potato or foreign object. Alternatively, if the horse is a greedy feeder it may be that dry feed is eaten too quickly and impacts in the gullet. Inadequately soaked sugar beet nuts may also cause this problem.

Ensure all food is prepared properly, carrots should be chopped into long fingers, sugar beet soaked thoroughly, dry feed given in small quantities.

Wood Chewing

May be as a result of insufficient long fibre in the diet, particularly when the horse is stabled and becomes bored. Ensure adequate roughage is available for the stabled animal and provide a salt lick to play with if boredom is the root of the problem.

If the wood chewing occurs when the horse is out at grass and not fed supplementary concentrates or minerals, it may be a symptom of mild phosphorus deficiency.

Chronic Obstructive Pulmonary Disease (COPD)

This is a respiratory problem caused by allergy to dust. The horse coughs, breaths with difficulty and cannot perform strenuous work. Some horses are particularly susceptible and therefore the best policy is to feed a dust-free diet. This may be achieved by soaking all hay fed (for approximately four hours), damping down feeds with moist products like soaked molassed sugar beet nuts or shreds or feeding comercially prepared vacuum sealed products such as Horsehage or Propack.

As most dust comes from the bedding , it is advisable to use an alternative to hay or straw, such as shredded paper.

These are the most common nutritionally related disorders you are likely to come across. Earlier in this chapter we discussed the importance of feeding the right diet, so that the mature horse neither gains nor loses a significant amount of weight. Perhaps you can now understand more clearly the need for a balanced diet as a large part of ill-health can be related to diet. The subject of nutrition is quite complicated but don't be afraid to ask for help from people who know the subject — often, that does not mean a friend or neighbour, but your feed merchant or a horse specialist. Urge him to give you accurate information on the feeds he is selling, both the analysis and the recommended rate of feeding.

Finally, a few key points to remember:

● Energy is the fuel and the more work done, the greater the energy requirements.

● Protein is the building block, hence do not overfeed mature animals in particular whose requirement for it is relatively low.

● Energy and protein are different nutrients and should be treated quite separately. Do not confuse one with the other.

● Remember the importance of clean, fresh water in the diet.

● Feed only one mineral/vitamin supplement at a time.

● Fibre is very important for the well being of the digestive tract and a healthy digestive system and a balanced diet means a happy, healthy horse.

Table 8
The fibre content and its digestibility coefficient of feeds commonly used in a horse diet.

Feed	Per cent crude fibre in dry matter	Digestibility coefficient (per cent)
Good quality hay	28-32	45-60
Medium quality hay	32-36	40-55
Timothy hay	30-34	51
Straw	39-55	29-37
Chaff	33	35
Wheat bran	11	42
Molassed sugar beet feed	14	66
Oats	12	25
Horse & pony cubes	8-14	not known

Ten ways to better feeding and health

Little and often — this way the diet is used more efficiently and helps to avoid dietary upsets. Grazing is the natural way which a horse feeds in the wild; small frequent meals are the closest and most efficient imitation of a horse's natural habit.

Regular routine — try to feed at the same time each day as the horse's mind and body expect the food at certain times.

Balanced diet — ensure there are adequate quantities of energy, proteins, fibre, minerals, vitamins and water in the diet. Over-feeding is as serious as under-feeding and can lead to poor performance and ill health.

Make sure your feed is kept away from contamination by vermin — keep it in metal bins and ensure these are out of reach of loose horses and horse proof. Mark the contents too, so that if someone else has to feed your horse for you they can make up the ration properly.

No sudden changes — either in the given amount or the ingredients. It takes at least one week for a horse to adjust to a new feed.

Appropriate feed programme — remember the more hard work done the more energy your horse requires. Do not confuse energy with protein, the two are quite separate nutrients and not interchangeable.

Water before feeding — if your horse does not have access to water all the time. This avoids your horse taking a long draught of water on top of a heavy feed which would impair the digestion of the feed by diluting the digestive juices.

Do not work fast immediately after a feed — as the full stomach will put pressure on the lungs and affect both breathing and digestion.

Feed adequate roughage — roughage is responsible for the well-being of the digestive tract. It stimulates the intestines and helps to break up concentrated feed which, when allowed to settle in the intestines, causes colic.

Good quality food — avoid any soiled, stale or mouldy feed which can lead to digestive upsets. Always store feeds in clean, dry conditions.

Likes and dislikes — closely watch your horse and establish its likes and dislikes, then if he shows any unusual behaviour you can act quickly to avoid problems.

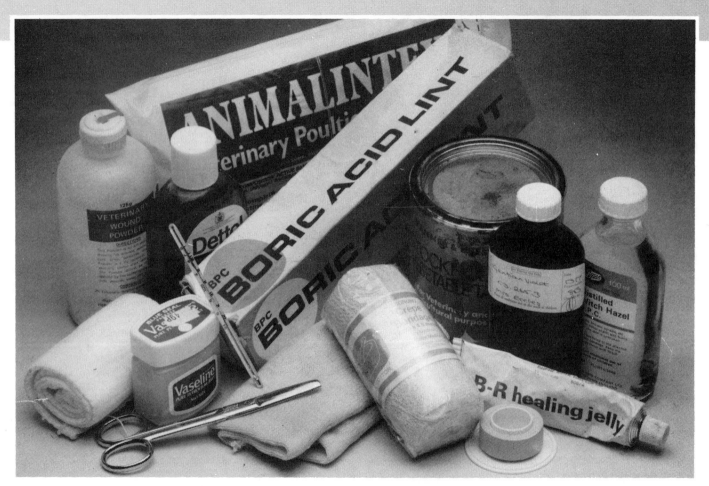

7. HEALTH CARE

Having your own horse gives you the chance to really get to know his character and habits. As well as being fun this information also comes in useful should your horse ever feel off colour. For there are various tell tale signs which let you know that a horse is not feeling well.

The ability to recognise these signs does not equip you to make a diagnosis however; they warn you that veterinary advice should be sought. Don't take chances with your horse's health — if anything is wrong get the advice of your vet. Prompt attention can save your pony unnecessary suffering.

Before you know whether anything is wrong you need to be aware of how a healthy horse should look.

Signs of Health and Disease

General attitude

Healthy animals are interested in their surroundings — they are bright and alert. At some point in the day you are likely to see your horse dozing in his stable or field. It is natural for him to rest in this way but he should not look listless or stand with his head lowered, looking dejected.

Certain conditions, like colic, cause the pony to be restless and uneasy. Behaviour like this, which is out of the ordinary, should ring warning bells.

Watch your horse at rest — most rest a hindleg at some time but never a foreleg. Horses which are lying down usually get up when approached — find out what is normal behaviour for your horse.

Coat

You'd expect the coat to have a certain amount of sheen — naturally grass kept animals are not going to look as good as stabled ponies. A dull, staring coat indicates that other symptoms of ill health should be investigated.

There should not be too much scurf and the skin should move easily. General malnutrition, lice and dehydration are shown by a tight skin.

Eyes

Bright eyes are a sign of health — if the eyelids are turned back the membrane should be a light, salmon pink colour. The linings of the nostrils should be the same.

Check any change in the membrane colour. A fever is shown by deep red membranes while yellow warns of liver disorders.

Pulse, Temperature and Respiration

Each pony is an individual so you need to know what is normal for your pony. A horse's temperature is taken within the rectum and is usually 100 to 101.5 degrees Fahrenheit.

115

Any deviation from the norm and you should consult your vet without delay. A rise in temperature of two or three degrees shows pain, above this it could mean a general infection.

At rest you should not be able to hear a healthy horse breathing — there should only be a slight movement of the nostrils and ribs. Respiration should be even and regular, at the rate of eight to twelve per minute.

If your horse's breathing is laboured it can mean pain, a temperature rise or pneumonia.

Check his pulse rate at rest — it should be between 35 to 40 beats per minute.

General Signs

Urine and droppings are also indicators to health — both are passed regularly by animals who are feeling well. A horse's urine should be light yellow — if there's a problem it may be thick and cloudy.

Although the colour of the droppings will vary according to the diet they should be formed into balls which break on hitting the ground.

Like people, sick horses will go off their food and drink. Make a point of noticing whether the water buckets have been touched and if the feed bowls have been licked clean.

Take the time to watch your pony eat — if he has trouble it could be that his teeth need rasping.

Preventative Measures

It's far better to try and stop illness occuring. Follow a sensible worming programme and have your horse vaccinated against tetanus and given annual boosters.

The tetanus injection can be combined with one for equine 'flu.

Sensible stable management ie good feeding routines, taking care that the horse does not catch a chill, generally observing your horse and taking prompt action when necessary, will help to keep serious problems at bay.

The First Aid Kit

Now you know how to recognise signs of health and disease but if you had to give your horse some first aid would you know what to do? Do you have the necessary basic equipment? Equally as important, do you know how to use the items in your first aid kit?

Let's have a look at this essential part of your stable equipment.

Bandages — two each of plain, elasticated and crepe should cover every emergency. Stable bandages are also handy for keeping dressings and bandages in position and clean.

Once the bandages have been removed from their packings keep them in polythene bags for cleanliness. Elasticated bandages are good for keeping dressings in place in awkward positions but if applied too tightly they can hamper circulation. You ought to be able to slip two fingers between the bandage and skin.

There are now specially shaped bandages to put on over the hock, knee etc.

Antiseptic — used, when diluted, to clean wounds as an antiseptic will inhibit the growth of germs. Use a bland one like Dettol. Also useful for sterilising bowls and thermometers after use.

Cotton Wool — used for swabbing wounds. Make sure it stays clean during storage.

Wound Powder — sulphonamide powder is an ideal dry wound dressing. If your horse lives out he will need a waterproof dressing over a cut — use the aerosol dressing which provide a protective film or the popular green oils.

Bowls — stainless steel kidney bowls are ideal for holding fluids, swabs and keeping instruments clean. They are also easier to sterilise than plastic bowls. Keep at least two in your kit.

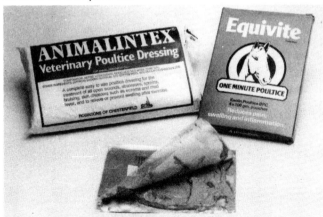

Ready made poultices such as these are a welcome addition to any vet kit.

Surgical gauze — for deeper wounds put the dry powder onto gauze and apply this to the cut. A cotton wool pad and a bandage will then hold the dressing in place. Don't use cotton wool alone as bits of it will stick to the wound. Gauze can be bought from chemists — you can get individually packed dressings for humans which are fine for your vet kit.

Scissors — blunt ended scissors are the safest.

Poultices — for speed and ease the best to keep are the ready-to-use poultices such as Animalintex or the Equivite One Minute poultices. The latter may be used hot or cold and are reusable.

Sponge — you may need to run cold water over a wound to clean it out or over a sprain or knock. Although this is easier done with a hose pipe there may not be one available.

Thermometer — available from your vet. Grease the end of the thermometer before inserting it into the horse's rectum. Make sure you wipe the instrument with a mild antiseptic before and after use.

Salt — useful for making up saline solution which can be used to clean wounds.

Tweezers — useful for holding swabs.

Water — it's especially useful to carry water with you as part of a travelling first aid kit which you can take to shows.

Cold hosing — a good aid to reduce swelling.

Keep your emergency kit in a marked box — it's a sensible precaution to include the telephone number of your vet and doctor too — write it on the lid. Don't forget to keep some loose change in the box for emergencies but make sure it is kept away from cotton wool, bandages etc, for the sake of hygiene.

Common Injuries

Wounds

No matter how careful you are there's bound to be a time when your horse cuts himself and you have to deal with the wound. Immediate attention is needed to stop the bleeding and prevent infection — if the wound is more than skin deep you should call the vet. It's worth taking the precaution of giving the horse an anti-tetanus booster anyway.

Tetanus is a killer disease which can be contracted through even the smallest of cuts.

There are four types of wound:

Clean cut — caused by a sharp edge such as glass, bleeding is usually severe.

Torn — as seen when barbed wire enters the flesh and is then torn out. Usually need stitching by a vet.

Bruised — the skin is not broken but the vessels underneath are ruptured.

Puncture wounds — caused by nails or thorns. Although the entrance to the wound is small the penetration into the tissues is usually deep, causing a serious problem. An abscess usually follows if the wound is in the foot and this has to be drained properly.

If your horse does sustain a wound the first priority is to get the bleeding under control, dress the wound and call the vet.

Bleeding may be venous or arterial. The first is when blood oozes steadily from the wound, from one or more veins. Pressure can be used to control venous bleeding — use a pad of cotton wool, a folded scarf or handkerchief. This can be bandaged over once the bleeding has stopped.

Arterial bleeding cannot be mistaken because bright red blood spurts out. This is quite common with a leg injury where the arteries are close to the surface.

Bleeding will be very heavy in severe cases calling for drastic action. A tourniquet should be applied over the artery above the wound, ie between the wound and heart. Pressure should be just enough to stop the bleeding but you should NEVER leave the tourniquet on for more than half an hour.

As you are stopping the bleeding so you are preventing the blood flowing to the other parts of the leg. After about 30 minutes the tissues starved of blood would die and gangrene would result.

RIGHT: Hocks are awkward places to apply dressings — use a bandage in a figure of eight for the best results.

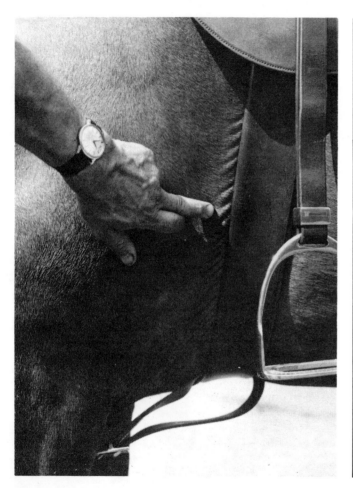

You should get someone to call the vet immediately and keep loosening the tourniquet at regular intervals until the vet arrives so that you do not interfere seriously with the blood flow.

To clean a wound clip away the hair around it, wash the wound thoroughly by trickling water onto it or using a saline solution, dry the wound and apply a dressing.

If you are calling the vet it's best to use a dry dressing as this is much easier for him to remove than oily, waterproof ones.

Do not probe about in the wound — if that is necessary leave it to the vet.

If bandaging is needed then do allow room for any swelling by putting on the bandage lightly.

Girth Galls and Saddle Sores

These injuries can put a horse out of action for several weeks yet are easily avoided.

Girth galls appear on the soft skin behind the horse's elbow and are caused by tight or hard girths. Bits of mud caught between the girth and skin can also rub.

Badly fitting saddles cause friction or pressure. As part of your daily grooming routine check for the early signs of any sores around the saddle and girth areas.

If there is soreness stop working the horse until it has disappeared. The wound may be open in which case it will need dressing.

Once the gall or saddle sore has healed you can

LEFT: this is how girth galls start as the skin is wrinkled by an over tight girth.

harden the skin by dabbing on saline solution or witch hazel.

Try to prevent a recurrence by removing the cause.

Bit Injuries

Riders with rough hands, worn or badly fitting bits can cause injuries which may show on the bars of the mouth, the tongue or cheeks. Stop work for a few days and sort out the cause. You can also wash out the horse's mouth with warm saline solution.

Injuries caused by interfering

Brushing and over reaching are two of the most common injuries caused by interfering, when the horse knocks himself on his legs or feet.

Brushing — this is when the horse's opposite limbs hit one another alternately, usually at the fetlock. Causes can be comformation faults, weakness or tiredness, or faulty shoeing. Young, unbalanced animals may also brush.

Find out why the injury is happening and, if possible, remove the cause. Animals with bad conformation will always be liable to brush so it's sensible to protect their legs with brushing boots.

Youngsters should wear protective boots too until they have gained more muscle when the problem is likely to disappear, providing it is not due to a fault of action or conformation.

Your farrier will be able to make feather edged shoes to help alleviate the problem.

Over-reaching — Galloping and jumping in heavy going can result in an over-reach injury. This is when the back of the fore leg, usually in the heel area, is struck by the hind foot. Sometimes the damage may happen further up the leg, injuring the tendons.

Usually the injury takes the form of a skin wound which can be cleaned and poulticed if there is some dirt which needs drawing out. Call the vet if the tendons or fetlock are affected as damage beneath the skin can be quite extensive. As protection your horse should wear over-reach boots.

Winter Problems

Horses have sensitive skins and in winter their natural defences can be lowered by the effects of the cold and mud. This provides an ideal chance for an organism known as dermatophilus congolensis to infect the skin.

Mud fever and rain scald are two of the problems caused by this organism. If your pony has mud fever the infection will leave the skin raw and oozing. Scabs form which must be removed to allow the skin to dry out. A mild antiseptic solution applied to the affected areas will kill off any remaining bacteria.

Ponies with severe cases of mud fever may be lame and need an antibiotic injection. During treatment they need to be rested and on laxative diets.

Stabled horses can get mud fever just as easily as ponies living out if their legs are not dried properly after mud is washed off.

Rain scald is a very different condition even though it is caused by the same organism. It is usually seen on horses which spend long periods out in the rain without rugs — their coats retain the water and the organism gains entrance to the upper layers of the skin.

The organisam burrows away, loosening the hairs — one of the early signs of this disease is wavy hair which falls out as you brush.

The hair does grow back but you can prevent rain scald by turning your horse out in a waterproof rug. If he lives out all year it's wise to have two New Zealand rugs so that if one does get soaked there's another to use immediately.

Another winter horror, which is also very painful, is cracked heels. The name is rather deceiving as it is the hollow at the back of the pastern which is affected. The skin here gets wet and chapped so becoming red and tender. Scabs form but when they drop off the hair is taken with them. The skin cracks open as the horse moves, enabling germs to enter and cause inflammation.

The infected area becomes swollen and the pony goes lame. Early signs to look for are itchiness, followed by scurf and scabs. Wash off the scabs and dry the area thoroughly, then apply zinc ointment or an antiseptic cream.

Left untreated the condition will last for weeks. For serious cases call in the vet — it's sensible to give the horse an anti-tetanus booster too as dirt could penetrate the wound.

Cracked heels are not caused just by the wet and cold. There are irritants in mud which can get into the skin if the legs are washed and then dried. It is better to leave mud to dry and then brush it off, rather than wash the legs, which removes the natural oils that keep the skin supple.

Bad stable management or neglect can cause thrush — a problem which is easily recognisable as the horse's hoof has a revolting smell.

Thrush affects the frog, causing it to become soft and spongy. A damp, smelly black pus infects the cleft and grooves of the frog.

If left untreated heat and lameness will develop. You need to wash out the hoof thoroughly, using water to which a strong antiseptic or disinfectant has been added and a stiff brush.

Dry the foot afterwards and smear on the old favourite, stockholm tar. Continue the treatment until the condition has disappeared and make a point in future of picking out your horse's feet daily and ensuring they are really clean.

Summer Care

See chapter 2 — Grass kept ponies.

Colic

One of the most common sicknesses in horses is colic — a disease of the digestive organs which can be fatal. Horses suffering from colic should be treated promptly by a vet.

There are different types of colic and most of them are the result of bad management or incorrect feeding. As with anything, prevention is far better than cure.

The quality and quantity of food you give your horse can cause colic. Musty hay, dirty food, too little or too much food can upset the horse's system. Bowel diorder will result from irregular feeding — one of the golden rules of feeding is little and often, in imitation of the horse's natural method. Horses love routine and will expect their feeds on time — if there are long intervals in between meals they will bolt their food without chewing it properly.

Another of the feeding rules, which if ignored, can cause colic concerns changes of diet. Any sudden changes, perhaps switching on to concentrates or putting the horse out on lush grassland, can lead to colic — always make any changes gradually.

Remember that water is as essential to life as food and clean fresh supplies should always be available. Sand in the stomach, caused by drinking from rivers with sandy beds, is another contributory factor to colic.

Sensible management including points like keeping the feed room bins horse proof, is the best way to avoid colic.

Spasmodic or flatulent colic is very painful but the least serious of the different types. It is caused by a collection of gas in the bowel which results in the bowel dilating leading to pain.

A stoppage in the bowel — perhaps of dry food or faeces, causes impacted colic. The most serious and usually fatal is that involving a twisted gut.

A horse suffering from colic looks uneasy and restless. They frequently turn round to look at their stomachs, breathe heavily and go off their food. Sweating and increased pulse rates follow, the horse looks in pain and may lie down and roll repeatedly. As the name suggests, in spasmodic colic, there are quiet periods and then times of great pain.

The instant you suspect colic call in the vet as only a professional should attempt to deal with this problem.

Worms — your horse's enemies

During summer the worm invasion begins — millions of worm eggs are deposited in horse dung on pastures. Of these a high proportion will develop into infective larvae which can cause all sorts of problems for our horses.

Weight loss, dry, staring coat, colic, tail rubbing, anaemia — these are just some of the symptoms associated with worms. Infestation by these parasites is obviously something to be avoided.

The main source of trouble is redworm or Strongylus vulgaris. If left to do as they please they can prove fatal, particuary to younger animals.

These worms have a relatively long life cycle, taking around seven months for the infective larvae to be swallowed by horses, reach maturity in the intestine and lay their own eggs to carry on the cycle.

It is as the larvae migrate through the horse's network of blood vessels and internal organs that they cause the most damage. They irritate and damage the arterial walls, causing blood clots and inflammation. If an artery is weakened it may rupture leading to death from haemorrhage.

The most characteristic sign of the presence of large Strongyles is colic but other pointers are diarrhoea, loss of appetite, weight loss and dehydration.

There are small redworms too, measuring about one quarter to two thirds of an inch as opposed to the inch long large Strongyles.

These usually occur in mixed infections and the main damage is done by the adult worm in the large intestine of the horse.

One of the best ways of controlling redworm is by following a sensible and regular worming programme. It's especially important to worm in the Spring when adult worms are laying their eggs in the horse. By worming you kill the adults and so reduce the numbers of eggs which are passed out onto the grass. Carry on with six weekly worming throughout summer and you'll be going a long way towards keeping your pasture safe.

The second of the two main types of worm to affect horses is the roundworm or ascarid. In adult horses they have little general effect but their presence can be serious in youngsters, especially those under six months old.

Ascarids are extremely resistant parasites — surviving for long periods outside the horse, they usually infect foals soon after their birth, migrating through the lungs. This can cause summer coughs and colds. Heavily infested foals become feeble, lose weight and have a pot bellied appearance.

As foals are so vulnerable to worm infection they need special protection. Their relatively delicate intestines cannot withstand heavy worm burdens and treatment should be started at six to eight weeks old, with regular doses every four to six weeks.

Bots have been mentioned under keeping ponies at grass — do remember to buy a wormer which deals with them.

One of the problems associated with having a donkey as a companion to a horse is the risk of lungworm. Strong wormers can deal with lungworm but if your horse has been with a donkey and develops a dry cough it is best to contact your vet and get expert advice.

Shoeing

One of the horse owner's greatest assets is a good farrier. Although their craft stretches back centuries today's practitioners are very much up to date.

Training as a farrier takes four years so you can appreciate how involved their task is — they are veterinary experts on horses' feet and how well your farrier does his job will affect the rest of your horse's working life.

It is your responsibility to see your horse's feet get regular attention. Every horse should be shod at six weekly intervals although some sports like long distance riding, mean that horses need shoes more frequently. Each horse is an individual and should be treated as such.

Horses which are not being ridden also need their feet trimmed as the foot grows continuously, just as human fingernails do. Unless your horse is doing only very light work on grass he will need shoes.

Every time you pick out your horse's feet check the condition of the shoes — are they loose or wearing thin Has a shoe been cast (lost)? Is the foot over long and out of shape? — this is another tell tale sign that a farrier's attention is needed.

Having decided that you need a farrier how do you find your local forge? As soon as you buy a horse ask at local livery yards, stables, saddlers — someone will be able to recommend a farrier.

You'll need to give reasonable notice that your horse needs attention as farriers with good reputations tend to be extremely busy.

Your horse may be hot or cold shod — the former is preferable. Someone who shoes cold carries a large variety of ready made shoes with him which are altered to achieve the best possible fit.

With the hot process shoes are made on the spot to your horse's individual requirements. To have your horse hot shod you may have to take him to the forge or the farrier may have a travelling forge so he can hot shoe on your premises. Ask him when you ring up for an appointment.

Prices of shoes seem to vary but do not expect to pay less than £16-£20 for a new set. If the shoes are not too badly worn the farrier can trim the hooves and replace them which obviously costs less.

Your shoeing bill is one area where you cannot afford to skimp on cost. You must shoe your horse regularly — if you don't take care of his feet you'll end up with a lame, out of work horse.

Shoe Types

Tell your farrier what work your horse is doing and he will fit the type and weight of shoe accordingly.

The most popular are the hunter shoes. These have grooved or fullered ground surfaces to give better grip and the heels of the fore shoes are smoothed off to cut down the chances of them being caught by the hind feet and ripped off.

There are shoes to help horses who brush, relieve pressure if the horse has corns, prevent the hoof wall from splitting and so on. If you have any particular problems talk them over with your farrier and vet.

Parts of the Foot

To understand the shoeing process you need a basic knowledge of the foot structure. The only parts we can see are the wall, sole and frog. When the horse's hoof is on the ground we can see the wall which is constantly growing downwards from the coronary band.

A horse's sole protects his foot from injury and is concave in shape to give him a better foothold. The V-shaped part on the underside of the hoof is the frog which acts an anti-concussion and anti-slipping device. As the horse moves the frog comes into contact with the ground first.

Should the wall, sole or frog be penetrated then the bones, sensitive tissues and joints within the hoof can be injured.

Shoeing process

By simply looking at your horse's old shoes a farrier can tell how to attend or 'dress' the hooves. He'll be able to see how the horse's way of going wears the shoes.

The old shoes are removed using a buffer and hammer. The clenches are raised and cut off, the heels of the shoe are eased with the pincers and the shoe is levered off.

Next the feet are prepared for the new shoes. Overgrowth of the wall is cut back with hoofcutters, and any ragged pieces of the sole or frog trimmed off with a drawing knife.

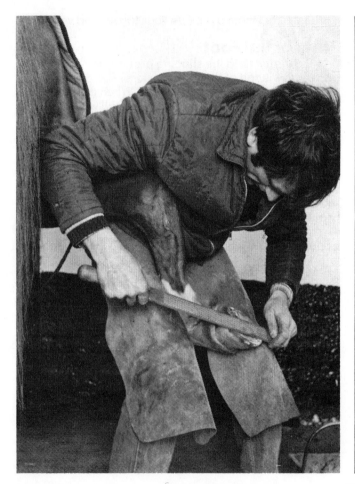

The surface is levelled with a rasp and small pieces taken from the toes to make room for the toe clips. So that the edge of the wall does not split the rasp is taken lightly around the hoof.

For a moment the new hot shoe is held against the hoof. The horn burns where contact is made and it is from these tell-tale marks that the farrier can judge how well the shoe fits and make any necessary adjustments.

When the shoe is perfect it is cooled and fitted. The nails are driven in, starting near the toe, usually with four on the outside edge and three on the inside. The number of nails used depends on the condition of the horse's feet.

Part of the nail will project through the hoof wall, usually about a quarter of the way up unless the horse has very shallow feet. This is twisted off leaving a small piece known as a clench. Small beds are made in the wall for the clenches which are smoothed and tapped down.

The toe clips on fore shoes and quarter clips on hind shoes are tapped back and finally a rasp is run around the edge of the wall to reduce any risk of cracking.

Studs

To give added grip, perhaps when jumping or for roadwork you need to use studs.

You must warn your farrier so that he can make stud holes in your horse's next set of shoes. Some studs can be left in but generally you only fit studs when you need them.

LEFT: Rasping the surface of the hoof level.

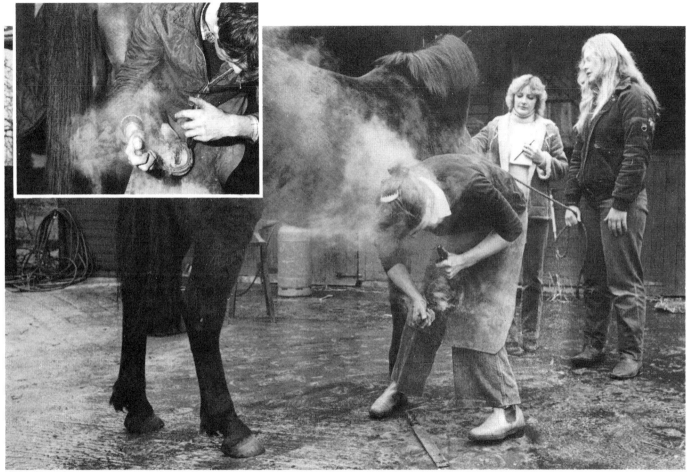

With hot shoeing a better fit can be obtained.

Keep the empty stud hole clean and clear by plugging and store the studs in a jar containing a little paraffin.

Lameness

Few horses get through their working lives without

some form of leg trouble — after all horse's legs especially those doing hard, fast work such as eventing, come under a great strain.

If you can recognise a problem or know how to avoid them so much the better. Perhaps you suspect that your horse is lame — how do you go about checking this out?

As lameness is an indication of pain most horses will try to avoid the pain by distributing their weight unevenly. Have your horse walked away from you and then towards you, on a hard, flat surface.

Then have the process repeated in trot — watch the horse's head which always nods when he's lame. Try to decide which leg he is nodding onto — this one will be the sound leg.

If both forelegs are moving freely look at the hindlegs. Watch as the horse is trotted away — one quarter will drop more than the other as again the horse drops more on to his sound leg.

Having discovered which leg the horse is lame on it's a case of pinpointing exactly where the problem lies. A higher proportion of problems occur in the lower legs, from the knees and hocks down.

However skill and experience are needed to diagnose lameness and of course, to know how to treat it, so it is wise to ask your vet's advice.

As you are riding you may feel your horse go lame. In this case always dismount and examine the foot. Your horse may have picked up a stone or a nail could have punctured his sole.

You may not be able to see the puncture mark but

any dirt which penetrates the foot leads to an infection setting in. Pus builds up and because the pressure cannot escape the pain becomes intense.

It is a skilled job for the vet to pare away the sole allowing the abscess to be drained. The cavity is washed out with antibiotic and the foot poulticed twice daily. It's essential to keep the drainage hole free of dirt and sensible to give the horse a tetanus booster.

Bruised soles may result from hacking out along stony tracks or by neglecting the feet so that the sole becomes flat or convex instead of being concave.

Shoes have to be removed, the bruised area pared out and poulticed. Rest is then necessary.

Another problem which can result from neglect of the foot is corns. Shoes left on too long or badly fitted cause a bruising of the sole between the wall and the heel.

Corns cause pain and lameness and may even affect the sensitive laminae and the bone. Treatment, carried out by the vet or farrier, involves removing the shoes, cutting out the bruised area and using special shoes to take pressure off the heels.

Should your horse go lame soon after a visit to the farrier it could be a case of nail bind. This is when a nail is placed too close to the sensitive part of the foot, perhaps causing a bulge of the horn and great pain.

Pricked foot is when a nail is driven at the wrong angle and penetrates the sensitive structures of the foot.

There is usually heat in the foot and the farrier should be called back to remove the shoes. With pricked foot it may take several days for the lameness to appear. Poulticing and rest are part of the treatment in both cases.

Sprains and Strains

An injury to a ligament is known as a sprain while tearing or stretching of the fibres of tendons or muscles is called a strain.

The fibrous tissues which connect the bones are known as ligaments while the fibrous cords which attach muscles to bones are called tendons.

The tendons at the back of the fore legs, behind the cannon bones are the most susceptible to injury. Imagine a horse being made to gallop or jump when unfit or tired. As his muscles are tired so they lose their elasticity and their ability to cushion the shock — the tendons then take the strain. Sometimes some of the fibres give way, in severe instances, the whole tendon ruptures. If this happens the whole tendon will 'bow' outwards. Seek the help of a vet immediately.

Injuries to the ligaments usually take longer to appear — brought on perhaps by concussion, or overwork. A horse's conformation may predispose towards strains and sprains too.

Treatment, as advised by your vet, and complete rest is essential.

Splints

These are bony growths which form on the splint bone where it connects to the cannon bone. Excess strain on the forelegs may result in a splint forming and as this happens the area becomes inflammed and swollen, often with some pain and lameness.

They usually develop in young horses, up to about the age of four years. Although the pain and lameness disappears the inflammed fluid and tissue change into bone.

Normally splints are found on the outside of the forelegs. If they form on the inside of the splint bone this is more serious as they can interfere with the action of the flexor tendons or the knee joint.

Treatment for splints varies from vet to vet but rest is essential until the lameness has gone.

Bone Spavin

This is usually referred to as 'spavin' and is a hard, bony swelling which develops at the front, inside and lower edge of the hock joint.

You will notice it when you ask the horse to walk out

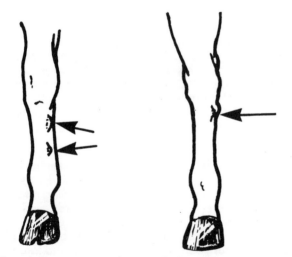

Left hand diagram — splints; right hand diagram — bone spavin.

from rest. Lameness will be evident as the horse shortens his stride with the affected leg and does not flex his hock properly.

A simple test for spavin is to hold the leg up tight to the horse's body for a minute or so and then have him trotted away immediately. If there is a spavin he will go lame for the first few steps.

The spavin may have formed because of strain, sprain, or injury. Rest is usually sufficient although in persistent cases a vet may advise blistering.

Bursal and synovial enlargements

Capped hocks and elbows, windgalls, bog spavin and thoroughpin all come under this heading.

The synovial membranes release a fluid called synovia which lubricates the inside of the joints, the sheaths which fit around the tendons and the sacs in various parts of the body called bursae.

Bog Spavin

This is enlargement of the synovial bursae when the membrance lining which controls the fluid secretion is damaged. An abnormal amount of fluid is built up and a swelling appears on the inside of the hock. It is in a higher position than a bone spavin.

Usually the swelling is soft and painless, the horse is not even lame. It is best to leave well alone but if there is heat and rest does not effect a cure then call in the vet.

Young horses are particularly vulnerable to these because of the elasticity of their joint structure — it can be caused by a blow or too much strain on a horse's hocks.

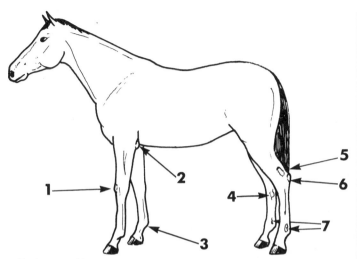

*1. capped knee **2.** capped elbow **3.** sesamoiditis **4.** bog spavin **5.** thoroughpin **6.** capped hock **7.** windgalls.*

Capped hocks and elbows

A blow to the point of the joint causes this condition, as the bursa become enlarged with fluid. Often they are caused by horses trying to get up from a stable floor with insufficient bedding.

Cold hose the injury and if it does not go down call the vet as he may have to drain off the fluid.

Thoroughpin

These occur at the back of the hock, showing as a lump either side of the deep flexor tendon just above the point of the hock.

Horses galloping through soft ground, rearing or kicking, may develop thoroughpin. It is treated in the same way as other synovial swellings.

Windgalls

Usually these appear in older horses. They affect both the fore and hind legs and are swellings around the fetlock joints.

Above the fetlocks are two tendon sheaths and when these become filled with synovial fluid windgalls form. The swelling feels soft and pliable to the touch but they are not an unsoundness, more a blemish and should be left alone.

Curb

Overworking young horses can result in curbs — sprains to the fibrous ligament between the point of the hock and the cannon bone.

The curb will extend down the inside of the hock and looked at from the side, it will curve outwards.

They can be quite painful, causing slight lameness. Complete rest is needed together with cold hosing. Once the horse is sound he must only be worked lightly for several weeks.

Sesamoiditis

This is inflammation of the sesamoid bones behind the fetlock joints. Faulty conformation, strain, turned out toes can all cause the condition.

Heat and lameness are usually present and rest seems to be helpful although there is no definite cure.

8. PREPARING TO COMPETE

Most horse owners like to compete — it gives them a goal to work towards and something to look forward to when braving the winter chills to exercise and care for their animal.

There's a variety of classes — from showing to ride and tie events, cross country jumping to long distance riding, gymkhanas to show jumping. No matter what sport appeals, you will have much more fun if you and your horse are properly prepared.

And time spent on schooling your horse will make him a much more pleasant and obedient ride on hacks too.

Regular schooling sessions, combined with hacks out, gymnastic jumping exercises and competitions will give a varied and interesting routine beneficial to your horse's education.

Allow at least one rest day a week so the horse can relax — Monday, after the exertions of the weekend, is a popular choice.

Schooling

If your horse is at livery you may be lucky enough to have the use of an indoor or outdoor school. If not, you can always rig up your own in a flat part of your field.

Mark out a large area with tyres or cans as four corner markers or ask someone who's handy with a hammer to make you a set of eight — each one about 18 inches square with a stake attached to the back so that it can be driven into the ground. These can be used to mark out a school — follow the lettering sequence used at your local riding school.

Keep a good balance between time spent in your school and out enjoying yourself because neither you nor your horse want to get bored.

The first few minutes in the school when you are warming up are important. You need to get your pony loosened up but paying attention to your requests. He should not be tearing around but trotting actively. If he is working and using his hindquarters properly he will track up — his hind feet will follow in the prints made by the fore feet.

So how do we achieve this? Work in walk and trot on both reins, keeping your work varied with plenty of changes of rein and changes of pace. If he does not answer to leg aids immediately, back them up with your stick. He must respond to your aids quickly, not when he feels like it.

Use large circles — 20 metres — as part of your work too. These are especially useful if the pony tries to rush on too much.

Always work in rising trot at first as your pony has only just come out of his field or stable. When he is warmed up give him a short canter on either rein to really loosen his back.

By this stage your pony should be going forwards nicely, be responsive to your aids and ready to do more complicated work.

Think back to the work you did at riding school — large circles, figures of eight, 10 metre circles, serpentines, different methods of changing the rein, turn on the forehand, rein back, starting on a 20 metre circle, decreasing the size to 10 metres and then increasing to a 20 metre circle again.

Don't forget to include transitions too — including halt. How about acute transitions — going straight from halt to trot, walk to canter? Count out your trot or canter strides as you go down one long side of the school, next time ask your pony to go on more and to lengthen his stride.

There are many different exercises you can put together to give your horse variety. If you can afford it have a weekly lesson on your own horse, then you will have the benefit of an experienced person pointing out areas which need improvement and suggesting ways in which you can achieve better results.

You can then work on the suggestions before the next lesson and will soon start to see an improvement. It is all too easy to develop bad riding habits once you have your own horse — even a monthly lesson is better than none at all.

Work without stirrups will help deepen your seat and improve your balance and feel for the horse's movement. There are plenty of exercises to be done on horseback — circling your arms and ankles, bending to touch your toes, lifting up your legs so you can feel your seatbones etc. Get together with a friend so you can help each other.

Why not use some simple dressage tests selecting various movements to incorporate in your schooling session?

Schooling need not always be within the confines of your schooling area. Practise transitions along bridleways and quiet lanes, try to perfect turns on the forehand as you open gates out on rides.

With a little bit of thought you can have a better balanced and more supple pony which will be advantageous in the competitive arena.

Gymnastic Jumping

Progressive and sensible preparation applies as much to those interested in entering jumping competitions as it does to everyone else. Success in show jumping is not achieved by clearing the odd huge fence the day before a show.

Much more thorough work is needed and it does not have to be at huge heights. Get your horse jumping well and confidently over small obstacles and he'll be able to gain the extra height on the occasions it's needed. If you overface and frighten him he will not forget and can easily lose his confidence.

Gymnastic jumping can be used for horses whatever their level of experience and are also useful for improving the rider's confidence and skill too.

A height of two foot nine inches will be fine for most of these grids, with the striding altered to suit each individual pony. If your horse is young be careful not to ask too much of him.

Work on a couple of exercises in each session — you do not want to tire or sour the horse. Always make sura that both horse and rider are happy before moving on to the next exercise. You'll find that as you progress you can run through some of the easier exercises quite quickly and use them as a warm-up for more advanced grids.

Trotting poles

These form the basic training equipment for anyone schooling a jumper. Start by walking and trotting over the poles, building up to six in a row. Usually the distance between poles is four foot six inches for trotting and a little closer if you are walking over them. Adjust any distances to suit your horse's stride.

You must bring your horse in calmly, on a straight

Gymnastic jumping is more beneficial than tackling the occasional huge jump.

approach and in a good rhythm. Remember to work on both reins.

Progressing to jumps

Once the horse is going well over trotting poles you can start to add small jumps. About nine feet from the last trotting pole place a small jump. Crossed poles are good as they draw the horse to the centre of the fence and the shape encourages them to lift and round more.

Try to jump out of a trot which makes the horse use himself more. Keep a good rhythm with the horse going forward clamly.

You can dispense with the trotting poles but retain one as a placing pole, about nine feet from the jump on the take off side. Using this helps to encourage the horse to jump off both hindlegs.

Gridwork

Small grids can be built to help the horse become more athletic. They can consist of all sorts of combinations — spreads, uprights, bounces.

Apart from teaching the horse to jump calmly and better, grids also sharpen up the rider's reactions.

In show jumping competitions the distances between fences conform to set measurements. However, this can be awkward if your horse has a particularly long or short stride. Through gridwork exercises you can teach your horse to go deeper into a fence, by altering the distances a little at a time, asking a short striding horse to stretch a little more each time.

Using bounce fences in grids teaches your horse to use his back and hocks. The usual distance for a bounce fence for a horse is twelve feet.

Single fences can also be useful — to achieve a rounder outline in the air, parallels of cross poles are used.

Again, it is worth having the occasional lesson and more if you can afford them.

Competing

When your horse is going calmly and happily over jumps at home it is time to try him out in a competitive atmosphere.

Clear round classes are ideal as a starting point providing the courses are built in a reasonable sized arena and the jumps made of decent poles and wings. Too often you see clear round courses built out of any old thing and crammed into a really small area.

You should expect to jump straw bales and tyres but draw the line at flimsy bits of wood. The object of these classes is to give you and your horse confidence before progressing to the main ring where it feels as if everyone is watching you!

Through the winter large numbers of riding schools have clear round jumping. Most people use them as schooling rounds and you have the chance to introduce your horse to new fences which you may not have at home.

Often they include a novice class at the end of the clear round which can be a good introduction to proper competition. Try to take your horse along regularly so he gets used to shows and learns to cope with the atmosphere instead of getting over excited at all the new sights.

Jumping Problems

If your pony jumped perfectly when you bought him but has since started to refuse or run out the chances are that you are doing something wrong.

Perhaps you have been overjumping him in your enthusiasm. If so, give up jumping for the moment and let him enjoy hacks out combined with some flatwork schooling. After a couple of weeks or so, just pop him over fallen logs or ditches when out on a hack. He should be happy to do these and then you can reintroduce jumping as part of your schooling. Remember to always keep a balance between anything you do or you'll have the same problem again soon.

Another reason could be that you are not presenting him at the fence properly and so not giving him a fair chance to tackle the jump. You may also not be very confident — the pony will feel any hesitation on the rider's part and begin to refuse. Have you been catching him in the mouth each time he's jumped? This will be painful and will soon put him off.

Having sorted out the problem you can look to putting it right. You have to learn to recognise your mistakes — there's no point trying to make your pony go over a jump if at each attempt you make the same mistake.

Refusing

You'd expect to have a refusal now and then but as soon as the first one happens you should immediately be working out why it came about and how to avoid it next time.

Inexperienced people often go too far away from

the fence before they present the horse for a second attempt. A pony can jump a small fence from a standstill if necessary so you do not need to go halfway across the field and come cantering in to your fence if it's only two foot six.

You need impulsion, not speed. If the horse is going forward properly in trot, is lined up squarely with the fence and you push him on determinedly there'll be no reason for a refusal.

Don't go miles away from the fence, three or four horse's lengths is enough . Aim at accelerating into the fence and think about urging your pony right over the fence, not just up to it. If you stop telling the horse what to do when you reach the take off point he isn't sure what you want so you cannot blame him if he stops.

Running out

Instead of stopping at his fences a pony may swerve off to one side and run out. Bring him round again, as you would after a refusal, but this time aim him at the opposite side of the fence to that side on which he ran out. Your pony must realise that you are the boss and that he must go forward when and where you tell him to.

Have your whip in the hand on the same side that he ran out. Often running out is the result of a poor approach on the rider's part so make sure you always present your horse correctly at a fence to give him every chance to make the jump.

Rushing

This is another common horse fault which can take weeks, even months to cure. The usual reason for horses rushing is incorrect riding or training in the early stages. If a horse has hurt himself over a fence in the past or he is in some pain then he will rush his jump to try and get it over with quickly.

You need to go back to basics and use trotting poles, small grids of poles and a fence as described in the gymnastic jumping section.

Work calmly, circling away if the horse starts to rush his fences and then quietly extending a circle to take in a jump once the horse has relaxed again.

Problems during the approach

Obviously the rider's ability to bring the horse in on a good approach will be a great help. If you get the approach wrong your horse may stop or run out.

If you have difficulty judging your line of approach practice over crossed poles which draw the horse and rider to the centre. Use both legs to keep your pony straight and look up between his ears.

By fiddling with the reins and over-checking during the approach you will destroy your pony's rhythm, balance and concentration so the jump will be poor. Ask someone to watch you jumping and to point out what you do wrong as you turn for a fence. You may not even realise that you are flapping and upsetting the horse.

Don't cut corners into a jump when there's no need. Against the clock you have to make sharp turns but first your horse has to be supple and balanced, as well as jumping confidently, to be able to cope.

Rider faults

A horse's bad jumping habits can usually be traced

back to the rider's technique. Before you even start to jump you should have developed a good position in the saddle and an independent seat so that you use your natural balance and do not hang on by the reins.

Instruction is advisable otherwise you probably won't know that faults are developing. If that isn't always possible ask a friend to take a photograph of you jumping — this can be very revealing!

The correct jumping position entails extending your hands further towards the horse's mouth so he can stretch without you jabbing him in the mouth; folding your body from the hips by thinking about pushing your stomach down towards the pony and keeping your back flat; keeping your head up and looking where you're

The correct jumping position.

going; seat bones close to but not pressing down into the saddle and taking your weight on the knee and thigh, pressing down into the heel.

Looking down to the side

By pulling her weight down to one side a rider unbalances the horse and may encourage him to strike off on the wrong leg on the get-away from the fence. Resist the temptation to look at the bottom of the fence or at your pony's legs. Pick out an object — a tree or similiar, to make yourself look ahead during the approach.

If you do look down that's usually where you go so keep looking ahead.

Standing in the stirrups

By doing this you are setting yourself against the horse's movement rather than sitting softly on top. As you stand you straighten your knee which should act as a shock absorber or cushion as you jump. If you stiffen your joints you will jar yourself and make your pony uncomfortable which can lead to him refusing fences.

Getting left behind

This is very uncomfortable for rider and horse. Instead of going forward with a horse's movement the rider tends to sit up straight. As a result the pony starts to jump with a flat back instead of rounding himself over the fence.

Dropping the contact

In the final strides of a jump the rider throws the

reins up the horse's neck so losing the contact with his mouth. Continually doing this can make the pony lose confidence in you. The rider needs to work towards gaining an independent seat and think of pushing their hands forward in the direction of the mouth.

Remember ...

● Do not interfere during the last three strides of a jump — it's too late to alter anything by this time. You should have everything in order and be telling your horse to go on.

● There's no point in trying to physically lift a horse over a jump — it doesn't do anything except lead to you standing in the stirrups which has its own problems.

● When warming up test your pony out by seeing if he does react to the leg as you canter down one side of the school or field. If he's not awake give him a reminder with your stick.

Getting your horse fit

Having decided to enter competitions or go hunting you need to get your horse fit. At some point in the year your horse should have a well earned holiday after which you must bring him back into work gradually.

You are aiming to convert flab into muscle and prepare the horse so that he can perform his work without injury to his wind, heart or limbs. At the same time as getting your horse fit you should be improving in fitness too.

The fittening process relates not only to exercise but to diet and stable management too. If your horse has never been fit, if he is young or has spent most of his life idling in a field, then it will take longer for him to reach fitness than for a horse who has been fit but let down and roughed off.

It's wise to check teeth and shoes and worm him before starting a serious fittening programme.

If your pony is already partially fit you can start further along this programme. If he's just had a holiday start with two weeks of walking, which helps to harden his legs. Hard or fast work at this early stage can damage his tendons and wind.

Start with 20-30 minutes of active walking, working up to an hour and fifteen minutes by the end of the second week. Then you can introduce short periods of trotting, gradually building up so they become more frequent and longer. This stage lasts for about three weeks, depending on the individual horse.

Walking and trotting requires the horse to use all his muscles but to improve his wind we must move on to faster work, via short canters.

By this time the horse is doing a couple of hours work which includes some schooling sessions. Hacking is not as energetic for the horse as schooling so adjust the time of work according to its quality.

For a horse who has been fit before an eight week programme is usually sufficient with the last couple of weeks including longer canters and some gallops at half speed.

This is only a guide — judge how your horse feels as an indicator of his fitness but bear in mind that highly strung types often appear fitter than they are. Do not mistake his jogging about for true fitness.

As a horse becomes fitter so his bulk food should decrease and the short feed increase

With a competition date in mind and fittening to be done always allow yourself extra time in case of any setbacks.

Exercise Problems

Being able to ride out your own horse whenever you want is probably one of the main reasons why you became a horse owner. But a new set of problems occur when the weather's bad — should you ride in snow? How do you cope with a soaking wet horse? What should you do in summer when the ground's rock hard?

In Britain we are lucky in that the climate does not seriously interrupt our riding for exceptionally long spells but there are times when a little common sense on the rider's part will benefit the horse.

Hard ground can be a problem in winter and summer. It doesn't matter whether it's sunbaked or frosty, the ground is likely to be rutted and uneven. With each step he takes the horse is forced to put his legs down at a slightly different angle. This puts strain on his joints and tendons — naturally the faster you ask him to go across such ground the higher the risk of him damaging himself.

Some horses are more susceptible to injury perhaps because of conformation faults — and especially so if you ask them to do work for which they have not been properly prepared. A horse's action is important — heavy cobs may pound the ground more and so the jarring effects of hard ground will be increased.

It makes sense not to jump or gallop too much when the ground is rutted — if you do take risks you'll have a lame horse and be unable to ride.

If you have access to an outdoor all weather surface you'll feel the benefit during a long hot summer or frosty winter. Something you can do if you are stuck for an exercise area is to lay out a straw or shavings ring in the field. Used bedding is quite adequate. It may only be big enough for you to lunge your horse but in winter it will be better than nothing.

Hacking out on the roads is fine in summer but icy surfaces are a different matter. Ask your farrier about fitting road studs but do not take uneccessary risks — if

Whenever you ride out you may meet an unexpected hazard — with a little encouragement you can persuade your horse to go forwards and pass the 'monster' which is all part of his education.

winter really sets in with a vengeance it's best to avoid riding out.

You still need to give your horse the chance to let off steam so turn him out if he is normally stabled. Before you bring him back in pick out his feet — a difficult job this as snow and ice will have become really packed — but it's vital otherwise he may slip on tarmac or concrete.

Whenever your horse is out of work — whether through weather conditions or illness — you have to reduce his hard feeds and when he's back in work adjust his fittening programme because he will have gone back a few steps.

If your horse gets wet when you're out on a ride you can dry him off by thatching him — putting straw underneath his sweat sheet and then placing another rug on top. You can also towel him to get him as dry as possible before thatching him but do not rub against the lie of the coat as you'll make matters worse.

Correct Dress

If you're new to competing the question of what to wear for the various classes can be puzzling.

Although there are certain accepted standards of dress for different sports it's important that you bear one word in mind each time you ride — Safety.

The hunting field for instance is one where tradition still plays a large part — yet with the increasing publicity on safety more and more people are wearing the chinstraps on their hats or using jockey skull caps with black silks.

Apart from protective headgear you should always wear sensible footwear. You need a heel to prevent your foot slipping right through the stirrup — so never ride in trainers.

General speaking you should aim to arrive at a show looking neat, clean and presentable on a tidy, well turned out pony.

Hacking jackets are fine for jumping, dressage,

Thatching a pony — use a sweat rug or a piece of old but clean sacking.

hunter trials, working hunter pony classes, handy pony competitions and so on. In a ridden pony showing class most people would be wearing blue or black jackets.

For showing in hand ordinary riding wear looks workmanlike — you do not want anything too flashy as the judge is supposed to be looking at the pony, not being dazzled by the handler.

At hunter trials the traditional dress is hacking jacket, shirt and tie but quite often you see people competing in jumpers rather than jackets and with skull caps and silks.

Tweed jackets are worn during cubbing but once the hunting season proper starts black jackets are worn by adults, children may wear hacking jackets. White stocks should only be worn with black jackets.

Competition checklist

Rider

Hat/jockey skull cap and silk
Back protector
Shirt and tie or stock and pin
Riding jacket
Jumper or rugby shirt for cross country
Jodhpurs
Boots
Gloves
Spurs (if worn)
Whip
Hairnet
Money for entries, schedule
Waterproof jacket

Food and Drink
Spare cash

Horse

Saddle and bridle
Martingale or breastplate if used
Protective boots for jumping/cross country
Travelling equipment
Headcollar and rope
Bucket and water (take your own water as your horse may refuse to drink strange water)
Grooming Kit for final touches
Rugs depending on the weather
Full haynet for the journey home if travelling by trailer/lorry
First aid kit for horse and human

Care after a Competition

After the excitement of completing a hunter trial or a long distance ride it's easy to stand around telling people about it instead of looking after your horse.

It does not take long to attend to your horse — it's simply a case of organising yourself and knowing what to do.

In summer your pony may be hot and sweaty after show jumping, playing gymkhana games and so on. Dismount, loosen the girth, run up the stirrups and lead him round until he's cooled off. It it's practical you may be able to sponge him down before walking him round.

Winter presents more problems as you need to keep your horse warm. Whether you're returning from a cross country event or hunting you need to dry your horse off before loading him, otherwise he could easily catch a chill.

Lead him round with a rug thrown over him until he has dried a little, then put his sweat rug on with his stable rug on top, the front of this rug being folded back over the withers. Secure this with a roller.

If your roller will fit over the rugs and the saddle so much the better — after being in the saddle for a long time it's wise to leave the saddle on so allowing the blood circulation to return to normal slowly. If you remove the saddle too quickly the blood rushes back and some of the vessels may be ruptured. Offer the horse a short drink of water with the chill taken off.

Check for any signs of injury which need immediate action — small cuts can wait until you get home and have everything close at hand unless you have a particulary long journey in front of you. Bandage your horse ready for travelling and load up.

It's a great help if you can muck out and prepare the horse's bed before going off to a competition — after a long day at a show the last thing you feel like is mucking out.

Once home remove the saddle and check the horse's condition — he may have 'broken out' ie. started to sweat again. To help dry your horse and keep him warm thatch him. This means putting straw under his sweat rug and then putting a stable rug on top for warmth. If your horse is prone to breaking out it's best to keep a couple of rugs spare so that the horse isn't standing in wet clothing. Put your stable rug on inside out as this will save the lining from getting damp — you can then reverse the rug when the horse is dry. Offer him water again.

If the horse's legs are still wet you can remove his travelling bandages or boots, cover his lower legs with a layer of straw and keep it all in place with a bandage. As you attend to the legs check them over for any thorns or injuries, treating them as necessary.

Your horse now needs to be left in peace, with a small feed. Do not give him his usual amount of feed yet as the digestive system of a tired horse finds it difficult to cope with too much. Some owners like to give a bran mash after competitions/hunting etc, while others prefer not to have such an abrupt change of diet. If your horse is a fussy eater he may not relish a mash.

If you want to make a mash half fill a bucket with bran, pour boiling water over it until its thoroughly wet, then cover with a sack and leave until its cool enough to eat.

After an hour or so check your horse again — he should be dry so you can brush off any sweat and dirt, checking as you do that certain areas, such as between the back legs where the skin is soft and more liable to become chafed, are really clean.

You may see people washing the mud off their horse's legs — it is preferable to dry them and brush the mud off later as this reduces the risk of mud fever and cracked heels.

Before you leave the horse for the night make sure he is comfortably rugged up — with a sweat sheet underneath his normal rugs if you think he may break out again.

After a day at a competition your horse deserves a rest the next day — perhaps a few hours in the field to relax and ward off any stiffness. If you cannot turn him out walk him out in hand and let him pick at some grass.

The world of equestrian sport is very varied and with such a wide choice it's possible to try out many different events.

This is beneficial to both rider and horse as it stretches their abilities and provides plenty of interest.

Show Jumping

This is now one of the most popular sports, with television coverage helping to bring it to the notice of millions.

In England this sport dates back to the latter part of the 19th century and by 1912 it was included in the Olympic Games. Eleven years later the British Show Jumping Association was formed, an organisation which today still organises and controls the sport.

Affiliated competitions are those run under the rules and regulations of the BSJA. At local shows you may find unaffiliated competitions which anyone may enter, subject to the individual rules as laid down by each show.

If you are successful in local shows you may wish to affiliate your horse. This will involve joining the BSJA, registering your horse and competing at affiliated classes throughout your area and beyond. Prize money won is recorded and you can upgrade your horse through the various stages.

You will know what type of course faces you according to the level of the competition but getting to the top in show jumping is difficult and costly. Not all horses have the scope to be top class, or the accuracy and consistency to produce good results all the time.

Show jumping is big business, with riders needing sponsorship if they are to compete at top level.

For those who do not aspire to such heights there is plenty of fun to be had in local competitions. Young riders can try for their Pony Club teams while older owners have the challenge of Riding Club teams.

Some people never go further than the novice classes at local shows because that is what they enjoy. The choice is yours.

Cross Country Jumping

For some the excitement and challenge of jumping and galloping across country holds more of a thrill than negotiating show jumping courses.

Good cross country courses have solid, well build fences with plenty of variety and alternatives to cater for the novice and experienced horses and riders.

You can choose between clear round cross country competitions, hunter trials and sponsored cross country rides with optional fences.

The clear round is run on the same principle as in show jumping. Many people use them to school their horses, introduce them to new fences they cannot practice over at home and build confidence. If they go clear their reward is a rosette.

You'll meet a wide range of fences — some will be natural obstacles such as hedges, ditches and streams,

others will be man made such as tiger traps, Irish banks and palisades. Those obstacles are fixed — they do not knock down if the horse hits them.

Some jumps will be part of the fencing surrounding a field, others will be out on their own, perhaps in the centre. These are known as island fences.

Most hunter trials and the occasional cross country competitions have a timed section. Your time through this designated area will be used to decide placings.

You may also have to open and shut a gate as part of the course in a hunter trial.

It is only by competing in these classes, or hiring the local riding school's cross country course that you can gain experience. Hunting does improve the way your horse goes across country but you'd be wise to have some cross country experience under your belt before going hunting.

Eventing

A sport which is highly demanding of both horse and rider is eventing. At the top level it requires extreme skill, courage and dedication together with plenty of time and money. There are however lower levels which can be enjoyed by everyone.

LEFT: Whichever level you compete at cross country jumping is an exciting sport.

RIGHT: Back protectors are cheap but wise safety precautions whenever you ride across country.

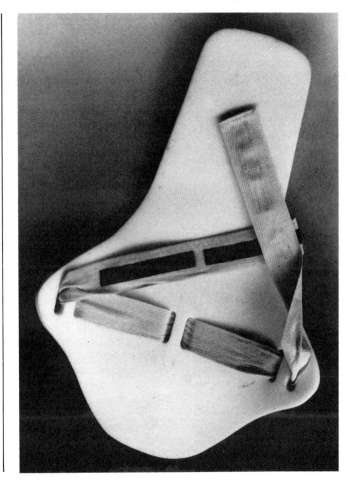

Eventing consists of three phases, dressage, cross country and show jumping. At top level the correct name for the second phase is speed and endurance as apart from a cross country course the competitors have to tackle two sections of roads and tracks plus a steeplechase course.

You'll find small one day events held by Pony and Riding Clubs, Hunt Supporters' Groups and riding schools. Your horse will have to be fit enough to complete all three sections in one day and the challenge to you as a rider and trainer is much greater as there are three disciplines in which you are tested.

Your marks for each section are taken into account to produce a final result.

Dressage

With the increase in riding to music displays throughout the country, dressage is being brought to the attention of the public.

The very word dressage seems to scare people off but there is no need. A dressage test is simply a set of school movements put together in a specific order. Many of the simpler tests involve nothing more complicated than circles, serpentines, canter work and some lengthening of stride.

You'll find that you do all these exercises as part of

RIGHT: International dressage riders and those on the lower rungs need to put in hours of work at home — this is Tanya Larrigan, a member of the 1984 Olympic team schooling at home.

your schooling — entering a dressage competition is a way of testing yourself. You can compare the judges' comments from test to test so you have an idea of how successful your horse's education programme is.

At the highest level dressage horses and riders present pictures of sheer beauty, elegance and harmony. While not everyone can attain those goals plenty of flatwork will result in a light, responsive horse, who's a real pleasure to ride.

Showing

Throughout the country there are hundreds of different show classes — from lead rein to working hunter ponies, in-hand classes to under saddle, side saddle to first ridden ponies, mountain and moorland to heavyweight hunters.

Most shows, even the smallest of the village events, have show classes. Tack and Turnout are a form of show class, as these are Bonny Pony and many other variations.

Why not start off in best turned out classes at your local show. It gives you the chance to put your presentation skills to the test — the judges are looking for well kept ponies who are clean, neat and tidy. Plait up if you can though native breeds and pure bred Arabs are not shown plaited. Make sure your tack fits well and is clean, your dress smart and appropriate. A discreet flower or rosebud in your jacket lapel adds a finishing touch but don't spoil the effect by forgetting to put your hair back in a net.

At the bigger shows you'll find in-hand and under

Showing classes call for a high standard of turnout of both pony and rider.

149

saddle classes. In-hand (led, not ridden) classes are for youngsters, brood mares with foals, stallions — divided of course according to age, sex, breed or type eg. riding pony type, show hunter. There are also some fun in-hand classes like bonny pony.

If you show your pony or horse you will probably have to do an individual show to demonstrate to the judge that the pony is obedient, well schooled and suitable for the type of class in which he is entered. The pony's conformation, action and manners will all be considered.

In a working hunter class you will have to jump a small course of rustic fences and your jumping is marked.

Long Distance Riding

Another of our growing horsey sports, long distance riding is something everyone can enjoy. You do not need an expensive horse or pony but you must be prepared to spend many hours in the saddle getting your horse fit.

Two organisations run long distance rides all over Britain — the LDR group of the British Horse Society and the Endurance Horse and Pony Society. Both organise pleasure rides of about 15 miles which serve as a good introduction to the sport.

Long distance riding involves covering a set course — perhaps 25, 50 or 75 miles with the final award depending on the average speed over the course and whether veterinary penalties were incurred. The overall condition and soundness of the horse is vital.

Long distance riding is a demanding sport which takes place in all weathers and in some of the most beautiful areas of Britain.

Before, during and after competitive rides the horses are vetted, their pulse and respiration rates taken and they are thoroughly checked over. If any horse is distressed it is withdrawn.

No money prizes are awarded — rosettes are gold, silver or bronze. To win a gold award a horse would need an average speed of over eight miles per hour. Bear in mind that you may be doing 50 miles over all kinds of terrain so keeping up this average leaves very little room for dallying.

There are also 100 mile rides which have to be completed in 24 hours. This sport does call for stamina, fitness and high standards of horsemanship and horsemastership.

No specific breed is essential although Arabs or those with Arab blood in them usually do well. Any horse, properly prepared, can try this sport. The ideal animal has strong quarters, good legs and feet, plenty of heart and lung room, a calm temperament (as he will be staying in strange places and with strange horses), and be able to cover the ground effortlessly.

Rides are held in Yorkshire, Exmoor, Wales, the Cotswolds and many other beautiful parts of Britain. You can travel as far as you can afford to and compete at whichever level you and your horse feel happiest.

Hunting

This is the oldest of the equestrian sports and is still very well supported. More and more people from all walks of life are hunting and enjoying the sport from which so many other sports have developed.

Any sport involves expenditure and hunting is no exception. If you wish to hunt regularly you must pay a seasonal subscription — anything from a hundred to several hundred pounds. It all depends on the hunt and how often you wish to attend — it is possible to hunt five or six days a week providing you have the horses and the cash!

Not all hunts can take new subscribers straight away — you may have to wait until an existing member drops out. An alternative is to hunt on a couple of occasions. Then you pay the hunt's current visitor's cap — again this could be £20, £50 or more. You need to contact the secretary first to ask if you may hunt with the pack.

Pony Club members can usually hunt for a much cheaper rate but the hunt may specify that the members has passed tests before they are allowed out without a supervising adult.

The season starts with cub-hunting when the young hounds are familiarised with their work, usually around mid-August or September — as soon as the harvest is over.

This is a good time to introduce young horses to the sport. The season proper starts on November 1st and continues until the end of March or early April, according to when the crops begin to grow.

Out hunting you are guests on other people's property and should treat it with respect. Don't go charging across crops, leaving gates open or generally making a nuisance of yourself.

The followers of the hunt are known as the field and the Field Master is in charge — he will tell you when to move off and must be obeyed. Each hunt has a Master or joint Masters who undertake all responsibilities from the kennels and the horses to organising the meets and public relations.

The hounds may be hunted by the Master or by a professional huntsman, assisted by the Whippers-In.

Always turn your horse's rear end away from hounds as they come past you — one of the cardinal sins is to kick a hound, the other is to overtake the Master or huntsman.

If you are not familiar with hunting first go out on foot and talk to some of the elderly country people. They are usually willing to help anyone who wants to learn.

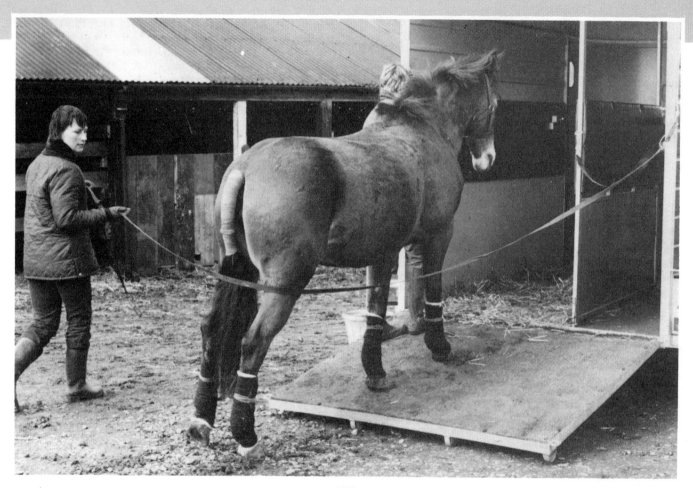

10. ON THE ROAD

As soon as you start competing transport for your horse will be vital. Although you will probably find some shows within hacking distance to compete regularly you will have to find some means of getting about.

The options are to hire, buy or find someone with transport who would like to share costs.

In some areas it is easy to hire trailers or horseboxes — investigate the possibilities in your district by checking the Yellow Pages, local newspapers and saddlers' notice boards. If you cannot find anything put an advertisement in yourself or contact your local riding or Pony club.

If you decide to hire a trailer there's the question of whether your existing car is capable of towing it plus horses — the hire firm may advise you, but if in doubt have a word with your local car dealer.

To hire a double horse trailer for the day you would expect to pay around £12-£15 plus VAT. If you need to hire a car as well the charge would be in the region of £40. To this you must add petrol costs and insurance which the hiring firm should be able to arrange.

You are unlikely to find someone who will hire out a horsebox for you to drive. Prices for a horsebox plus driver may be per day or per mile. Ask about VAT and insurance too.

With these costs in mind it is cheaper in the long term to buy your own transport, especially if your present car is capable of towing a trailer. Most one horse owners opt for trailers rather than keep a horsebox and a car for everyday use.

For a new trailer the outlay will be in the £1500-£2000 range. There are several trailer manufacturers so compare the various models and the facilities offered for the price.

Double trailers are preferable to single ones even if you have only one horse. You may find someone to share costs anyway. A front unload facility is better than having to back the horses out.

Try towing a trailer before you buy so you have an idea of how it handles behind your car.

Secondhand trailers are often advertised in local newspapers or the equestrian press. Prices vary according to age and model. If it's been well looked after an old trailer will still give years of service but you may find they are heavier than the more recent models.

With secondhand vehicles one of the major priorities is a sound floor. Test it by jumping up and down on it, look for any rotten wood or any previous repairs. Replacing a trailer floor can set you back in terms of time and money.

Check the condition of the bodywork, including underneath; that the electrics are safe and in working order; that the tyres are legal — again anything which needs replacing adds to your costs so bear this in mind when negotiating the price.

Look at the ramps — do they need new matting? What about the inside — are the partition and breast bars still sound?

Take care of your trailer — muck it out each time it's used and make regular maintenance checks.

New horseboxes are in a different league, costing

several thousand pounds. You can pick up older ones for much less but be prepared to spend money on repairs and if possible take a mechanic along when you view the box.

Before you go ahead and buy anything it is wise to check that your horse will load. Some animals are only happy in a horsebox, others will travel in either trailers or lorries.

Hire or borrow a trailer first — you may find your 15.3hh cobby type doesn't want to know about standard size horse trailers but will happily go in larger ones intended for 17 handers!

Towing

If towing a trailer is new to you make sure you have plenty of practice, away from the road and without the pony — there's no point in subjecting the poor animal to your mistakes.

To gain experience drive around quiet areas — perhaps an industrial estate on a Sunday when there's very little traffic around. When cornering always take a wide line so the trailer wheels do not bump over the kerb and remember the extra length and width.

Going forwards is comparatively easy but reversing is different again. You'll need to practice this much more before venturing out. The difficult part is getting used to turning the steering wheel in the opposite direction to that of the corner initially.

This gets the trailer turning correctly and you then steer as normal. The actual point when you change over causes problems — if you go too far with the steering one way it is difficult to correct. If this happens it is usually easier and quicker to pull forward and try again.

Remember to give yourself extra room when cornering and overtaking with a trailer otherwise this will happen.

154

With more up to date trailers you can simply reverse when necessary but with older versions you have to flick over a trailer reversing catch.

For towing it's wise to fit your car with door or wing mirrors on both sides. Most cars have off side exterior mirrors but if your vehicle is an older one it may not have a nearside mirror. It makes life much easier if you can see the trailer clearly.

Each time you see the trailer check that all the lights are working. It should have the same lights as the tow vehicle — two rear lights, indicators, brake lights and some form of number plate illumination. Trailers first used after 1980 should have rear fog lamps too. Two rear reflectors (red triangles) should also be standard and side lights on the wings if the trailer is wider than the tow vehicle.

Your trailer dealer, motoring organisation or the police will advise you about your speed limits and conditions if you are in any doubt.

You will probably find that your trailer has to be insured as an extra to your car policy. Your horse needs to be insured too.

Your horse's travelling equipment

However short the journey it is worth protecting your horse from possible injury with the correct boots and bandages.

A poll guard — usually a roll of sheepskin — on his headcollar is particularly important if the horse tends to throw his head up as you lead him or during travelling.

There's now a wide range of boots which are easily and quickly fitted to the horse's lower legs. For long journeys though, travelling bandages over gamgee or some other form of padding, offer more support.

Knee caps and hock boots are also worn together with a tail bandage and tail guard. Rugs may be needed depending on weather conditions.

Loading problems

Trouble-free travel makes show days so much more enjoyable so if your horse is not the best when it comes to loading and unloading you need to work on the problem well in advance.

There's nothing more infuriating than being ready to go to an event and the horse digs his toes in at the bottom of the trailer ramp. Your horse should walk in without any fuss whenever you want him to — whether it's on a busy showground, after hunting or at home.

Expect to have to spend quite a long time getting your horse accustomed to loading so that it is as routine to him as going into his stable.

Brute force will not get you anywhere — you'll only succeed in upsetting yourself and your horse. There may be a very good reason why your horse is reluctant to load — possibly an accident in the past — so you may find you have to go back to square one.

Your horse has to realise that the trailer is not a nasty object and to associate it with pleasant experiences.

Make the trailer as inviting as possible — move over or remove the centre partition, open the front unload door to give more light, spread plenty of straw inside, put the ramp stabilisers down.

Walk your horse up to the ramp and have a positive attitude yourself. You may find that the horse who has never loaded before will walk up totally unconcerned. He'll more likely stop and investigate the ramp — let him have a good look and sniff. Ask a helper to stand to the side of the ramp or just inside the trailer itself with a bucket and some pony nuts. try to tempt the horse a little further up the ramp with this.

Horses are individuals and some will happily put their feet on the ramp the first time and move up a little while others will not. This is where patience is necessary, spend time each day encouraging the horse to go a little further into the trailer, do not try to rush things.

When he does as you ask, reward and praise him. Always finish the session on a positive note — if the horse is an awkward loader you may have to 'sit it out'. For instance the horse may decide one day that he's not going to put his feet on the ramp, having cheerfully spent the last four days standing almost in the trailer! Don't let him get away with this — but don't turn it into a battle — you'll lose. Keep your cool and coax him until he gets bored and puts his feet on the ramp again.

To avoid going into the trailer a determined horse may dash round the side of the ramp. Always be prepared — position the trailer against a wall or fence and use a bridle for more control.

Do not rush your horse or fight him — learn to outwit him, especially in the case of horses who have no reason to worry about trailers but are simply being stubborn.

Some people advocate placing the trailer in front of the stable door so that the horse is channelled from the stable into the trailer with no escape route. This does work but some owners prefer not to invade the 'security' which a stable offers to its occupant.

When you are coaxing your horse into the trailer there's no harm in lifting up his feet and placing them on the ramp. Providing he doesn't kick, two volunteers may get results by linking arms around the horse's quarters and heaving, while giving vocal encouragement. This is usually more successful with small ponies than bigger animals.

A similar method can be used on horses which kick but to spare your helpers attach two lunge lines to the trailer crossing them above the horse's hocks.

If you're stuck on your own with a reluctant loader attach a lunge line to the headcollar and pass it through the tying ring inside the trailer. You can then use this as a pulley and stand at the free side of the ramp to stop the horse escaping to the side.

Surprise is another useful element which is why the water trick sometimes works. This involves splashing water onto a horse's quarters as he is standing square on the ramp — the shock sends him forward. Only a little water is needed and it should be reserved for the really awkward creatures. It's only likely to work once as well.

There's no doubt that to be really successful you have to use a long-term method and then, having persuaded your horse that the trailer isn't to be feared, ensure that he keeps that view. Always drive considerately, keep the trailer well maintained, make loading and travelling a pleasant experience.

RIGHT: *Should you ever be in the unfortunate position of being on your own and with a difficult loader try putting the lead line through the tying up ring so the horse is pulling against himself. It works like a pulley system and is usually successful.*

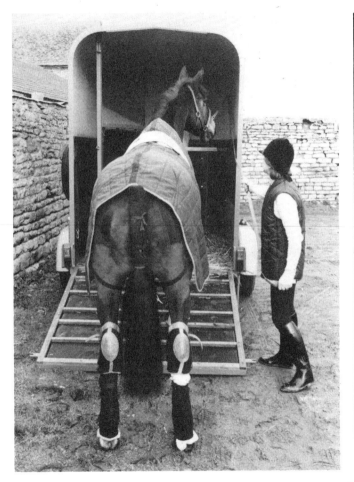

Don't let your horse charge off when you unload him and practice unloading by backing him out as you may not always have the facility of a front unload trailer.

For safety's sake wear gloves during all loading processes as rope burns are very painful; wear a hard hat as the horse may suddenly rush into the trailer and could knock you over; finally never wrap the lead rope around your hand as you are again inviting injury.

Road Safety

After riding in indoor arenas or going out on escorted hacks it's quite an experience for the new horse owner to ride out alone. With the increasing amount of traffic it's necessary to know how to ride properly and safely on the roads.

The British Horse Society run a Riding and Road Safety Test which anyone over the age of ten can take. Contact the BHS for details of your nearest exam day and ask about their booklet "Ride and Drive Safely" on which the tests are based.

Eight accidents involving horses happen every day so it's well worth finding out how to behave on the roads. Some tips follow but to make sure you're really safe — take the test.

The test will be in three parts — theory, simulated road route and a road test. The simulated test will be in a field, with 'roads' marked out using cones and including hazards such as a parked car. If you can cope with this section you will be allowed out onto the road, probably around a village where a route has been marked.

The examiners will look for thinking riders who can control their mounts and show consideration to others.

● To turn right —

Always ride on the lefthand side of the road and well before the junction look behind over your right shoulder, transfer your whip into the left hand and signal, with your arm out straight and your palm facing the front.

Halt at the junction, look right, left and right again. If it's clear walk purposefully on, aiming for the edge of the road before turning.

● To turn left —

You must remember to look behind, signal clearly and halt at the junction, then move off steadily.

● Dismounting and leading in hand —

You'll be asked to do this so make sure you know how to mount and dismount properly — try not to let nerves get the better of you or you could find yourself mounting on the wrong side!

You should pull into the side of the road, dismount as usual, run up the stirrups and prepare to lead your pony. If he has a martingale the reins should be left where they are, if you do not use a martingale then bring the reins over his head to lead him.

Remount as usual but always remember to look behind and signal before moving off.

● Hazards

These may be parked cars, roadworks and so on. Look behind as you approach the hazard, give a clear signal and move into the centre of the road to pass the hazard. You should have both hands on the reins as you pass. If the hazard is a parked car watch out for

Whatever your age the Road Safety test will benefit you and your horse.

158

passengers or dogs who may frighten your horse.

Be prepared for any spooking by turning the horse's head away from the hazard as you pass and keep your right leg on to keep the horse's quarters in.

REMEMBER

● Thank drivers who slow down or stop for you — courtesy costs nothing.

● Read the Highway Code.

● Wear proper clothing at all times.

● Talk to your horse as this often reassures and soothes them if something is likely to frighten them.

● If you catch up with other riders ask if you may pass them and do so sensibly.

● Look, listen and think ahead at all times, be aware of possible hazards.

● Ride on verges wherever possible but not on ornamental verges, gardens or footpaths.

● Do not try to pass frightening objects when traffic is approaching you.

● Do not dismount unless it is absolutely essential and never lead a pony by wrapping the reins around your hand — you could easily be dragged if the pony is startled and runs away.

● Remove any earrings before you ride.

Signalling clearly and checking for traffic during the road test section of a Riding and Road Safety examination.

11. ADDRESSES

Arab Horse Society
Goddards Green,
Cranbrook,
Kent, TN17 3LP.

Dales Pony Society
Ivy House Farm,
Hilton,
Yarm,
Cleveland, TS15 9LB.

Dartmoor Pony Society
Weston Manor,
Corscombe, Dorchester,
Dorset, DT2 0PB.

English Connemara Pony Society
2 The Leys,
Salford,
Chipping Norton,
Oxfordshire.

Exmoor Pony Society
Quarry Cottage,
Sampford Brett,
Williton,
Somerset.

Fell Pony Society
19 Dragley Beck,
Ulverston,
Cumbria, LA12 0HD.

Highland Pony Society
Rowan Cottage,
Meigle,
Blairgowrie,
Perthshire, PH21 8RH.

Irish Draught Horse Society (GB)
4th Street,
National Agricultural Centre,
Stoneleigh,
Warwickshire, CV8 2LG.

New Forest Pony & Cattle Breeding Society
Beacon Corner,
Burley,
Ringwood,
Hampshire, BH24 4EW.

Shetland Pony Stud Book Society
8 Whinfield Road,
Montrose,
Angus, DD10 8SA.

Welsh Pony & Cob Society
6 Chalybeate Street
Aberystwyth,
Dyfed, SY23 1HS.

British Horse Society
British Equestrian Centre,
Kenilworth,
Warwickshire, CV8 2LR.